John [illegible], on his [illegible] May [illegible], 19[illegible]

from Mom and Dad

U★S
NAVY
RICHARD HUMBLE

U★S NAVY

ARCO

First published in the United States of America by
Arco Publishing, Inc.
215 Park Avenue South, New York,
N.Y. 10003, USA

Produced by Winchmore Publishing Services Ltd,
40 Triton Square, London NW1 3HG, England

ISBN 0 668 06163 4

Designed by Roy Williams

Printed in Yugoslavia

CONTENTS

1: BIRTH OF A NAVY 1775-1798

When a new or reconstituted nation decides that its security and prosperity depends on maintaining an ocean-going navy, the results are liable to be as far-reaching as the oceans themselves. Over the past 120 years, culminating in the two World Wars of the 20th Century, this has certainly been the case with the new navies of Italy, Germany, and Japan. Remembering their influence on the Second World War alone, the creation of an ocean-going Soviet Navy since 1945 has been a most ominous accompaniment to the rapid decline, after centuries of paramountcy, of British sea power, the world's strongest until the postwar relinquishment of Empire.

The mantle of global naval supremacy passed from the British to the United States Navy 40 years ago, in the latter years of the Second World War; and fortunately for the Free World the United States Navy remains the world's strongest in the 1980s. But the origins of American sea power present a startling contrast to the 'instant navies' so eagerly created by Italy, Germany, and Japan in their demand for recognition as world powers. Far from being an aggressive or nationalist demand for a 'place in the sun,' the creation of the United States Navy in the last decade of the 18th Century was a grudging, reluctant acceptance of unwelcome necessity. And this is all the more surprising because the United States only emerged as a new nation after successfully defying the most renowned naval supremacy since the Roman Republic defeated Carthage.

When resistance to the force of British arms began in the American 'Thirteen Colonies' in the spring of 1775, only a minority of American activists really believed that total independence from British rule was their true goal. There was little to indicate that 200 years later the colonists' descendants would be citizens of the world's most powerful nation, possessed of the strongest armed forces on the planet. Indeed, in 1775 this was virtually the status of Britain, whose control the American colonists felt driven to challenge. Only 12 years earlier, Britain had emerged as the victor in the first true world war: the Seven Years War (1756-63), which had seen France and her allies confounded in land and sea battles from Canada to Bengal. As British subjects, the American colonists had played their part in that victory, on land against the French and their surrogate Indian 'troops' in Canada, and at sea as privateers preying on French trade. The Colonies had also supplied some

18,000 seamen to the Royal Navy. In its origins, the War of American Independence should be seen as a violent series of strikes by the colonists against what they saw as arbitrary and unfair taxation to pay for a war which they had helped to win, and against the garrisonning of regular troops on American soil (also to be paid for by the colonists) to enforce British authority.

In 1763 the 'Thirteen Colonies' consisted, from south to north, of Georgia, South Carolina, North Carolina, Virginia, Maryland, Delaware, Pennsylvania, New Jersey, New York, Connecticut, Rhode Island, Massachusetts, and New Hampshire, the latter extending up to French Canada and including what later became the State of Maine (in 1820). Together they amounted to a settled land area of around 250,000 square miles (almost three times the size of England and Scotland) inhabited by about 1.25 million colonists of European descent or birth, with about 250,000 negro slaves – already an impressive population compared with the 7 million of Britain. The era of purely English emigration to 'The Americas' was long gone, and by the early 1770s America's population was swelled by many Irish, Scottish, German, Dutch and Scandinavian families. Since 1717, there had also been repeated shiploads of English convicts dumped or 'transported' to the New World colonies – in theory for hard labor until their deaths but more often than not, as in Australia in the following century, to begin new lives on and behind the steadily expanding colonial frontiers.

Convict transportation, incidentally, was another anti-British grievance harbored by Americans. 'What would you say if we were to transport our rattlesnakes to England?' was the famous protest of Benjamin Franklin. But it helped swell a population containing many elements – the Irish and Scots to the fore, not to mention the jailbirds – naturally ill-disposed to put up with high-handed decrees from the King of England's haughty ministers. The growing cities of the Atlantic 'Tidewater' already boasted their own aristocracies and snobberies; the colonies contained thousands of 'Loyalists' who later moved to British Canada rather than endorse American independence. In the main, however, the colonies of America contained a potent human brew which spurted to defiance under the pressure of British governmental obstinacy, misplaced contempt and woeful miscalculation. If pushed, they were ready to fight – and that included an increasingly numerous and confident seafaring population, merchant traders, whalers and deepsea fishermen, operating out of ports along a thousand miles of coast between New England and the Carolinas.

After the defeats which the Royal Navy had inflicted on the navies of France and Spain in the Seven Years War, the prospects for American colonials seriously challenging British sea power were almost ludicrously bad – when measured in terms of heavy warships, custom-built for decisive fleet actions. Of these the colonists had none, nor any experience in building them or casting heavy guns. But commerce warfare, hitting at British merchant shipping, was a very different story. Even the lightest vessel able to cruise the Atlantic, though armed with the most modest array of guns, could achieve successes out of all proportion to the number of merchantmen it might capture or sink. Such attacks would force the British Admiralty to sail merchant ships in convoy, dislocating the normal pattern and profits of Britain's merchant trade and sending costs soaring; warships detached to escort convoys would be unable to blockade American ports or attack American shipping.

Commerce warfare of this nature was ideal for the Americans, being cheap and easy to wage. It could be entrusted to privateers: armed vessels manned if necessary by their normal civilian crews motivated by a personal stake in the plunder, licensed by 'letters of marque' authorising them to take prizes from a designated enemy. A commerce war waged by privateers, with the patriotism of their skippers and crews sharpened by the profit motive, could enable the Americans to wage a highly effective naval campaign as far as British home waters. If there seemed little chance of American victory in an all-out land and sea war with Britain, there was still every chance of pressurizing the powerful British merchant interest into joining the sympathetic voices advizing a settlement with the indignant colonies. Every colony from which ocean-going ships put to sea could contribute to such a campaign, which could well be a long one. Though British naval countermoves could be expected to inflict heavy losses, American shipyards had the capacity to replace every privateer captured or sunk. By 1775, Massachusetts alone was turning out 150 ships a year, and American shipbuilding was becoming more economic than in England (£2,600 for a 200-ton ship built in Philadelphia; £3,000 for an equivalent vessel built on the Thames).

As the cheapest and easiest method of waging maritime war against such a powerful naval opponent as Britain, privateering could be conducted on a single-ship basis by individual colonies. For anything more ambitious – even the smallest armed squadron capable, say, of tackling an escorted convoy or raiding British island possessions in the Caribbean – inter-colonial collaboration was essential, if only because of the limited supply of guns in the colonies. Because of this, privateering remained the most important American strategy against Britain in the War of Independence and the succeeding War of 1812, 30 years later.

The events leading to the first shots in the War of Independence were complex, but may be briefly summarised here. In their first attempt at concerted action against British taxation, nine of the 13 colonies sent delegates to the 'Stamp Act Congress' which met at New York in October 1765. Unprecedented as it was, this disconcerting display of colonial solidarity achieved the repeal of the hated Stamp Act in March 1766, but only led succeeding British governments to seek other ways of showing the colonies who was master. The fateful catalyst was the British attempt to rescue the failing East India Company by 'dumping' its surplus of tea, taxed at the full rate and sold only by carefully selected agents, on the American colonies. This was in the autumn of 1773, and when the first shipment of tea reached the ports of Charleston, Philadelphia, New York and Boston it was to encounter a mixed campaign of passive and active resistance. The humiliation of being used, financially exploited to bail out a British company, had resulted in outrage in the colonies, carefully orchestrated by 'corresponding committees.' The tea unloaded at Charleston was stored in cellars, with not an ounce sold. At New York and Philadelphia the ships were refused permission to unload and returned to Britain with their cargoes. At Boston the world knows what happened: the ships were boarded by demonstrators of the 'Sons of Liberty,' disguised as Indians, and the tea dumped into the harbor. The 'Boston Tea Party' of 16 December 1773 established Massachusetts, and the port of Boston in particular, as the center of colonial obduracy, to be chastized by economic pressure and if need be by military force.

The ensuing British 'Coercive Acts' of early 1774 were aimed at forcing Boston to make full restitution for the 'Tea Party,' but also intended effectively to place Massachusetts under much tighter political control. The Acts led to the summoning of the 'First Continental Congress' at Philadelphia in September 1775. Attended by 56 delegates from 12 of the colonies (all but Georgia), this second colonial congress rejected the Coercive Acts as unconstitutional and promised support for Massachusetts in ignoring them. Massachusetts was advized that it should form its own elected government, collect its own taxes and run its own revenue – and arm itself with a citizen militia to resist further attempts at coercion. The Congress finally drew up a 'Declaration of Rights and Grievances' for the edification of King George III, and approved an American boycott of all British goods to help this petition to bite. May 1775 was set as the date for Congress to reassemble, if American grievances had not been redressed in the meantime.

All this dictated the way in which the war broke out in the spring of 1775. Massachusetts stood out as the number-one troublemaker, and the enthusiastic recruiting of the Massachusetts militia was an obvious direct challenge to the 4,000 British troops in Boston. General Gage, Military Governor of Massachusetts, did what he could to lessen the threat by seizing all arsenals and ammunition depots likely to fall into colonial hands. One of these attempts sent 800 British troops from Boston to Concord in April 1775. On 19 April 'the shots heard round the world' were fired against 70 militiamen at Lexington, with the British marching on Concord after a heartening skirmish which had cost them one man hit in the leg, eight militiamen dead and ten wounded. The day ended with the British fighing a miserable and costly retreat back to Boston, sniped at all the way by militiamen, and an aggregate British loss of 73 killed, 174 wounded and 26 missing. American losses were only 49 killed, 41 wounded and five missing. By the end of the month, Gage's men in Boston were hemmed in by 15,000 militiamen from all over New England.

There never was a hope of confining the flare-up of colonial resistance to the Boston region. On 10 May, 170 miles away to the north-west, Colonel Benedict Arnold of the Massachusetts militia and Ethan Allen's 'Green Mountain Boys' rowed across Lake Champlain and caught the British garrison

of Fort Ticonderoga completely by surprise. Two days later, 10 miles further north, Fort Crown Point was taken as well. Rough and ready though it was, this was an inspired stroke, severing the British in Boston from any hope of prompt overland relief from Canada. Gage could only hold on at Boston and await reinforcement by sea, with his troops controlling no more than the ground they stood on – and hope that the colonial delegates who convened the 'Second Continental Congress' at Philadelphia on 10 May would fall out.

But the second Philadelphia Congress did no such thing. It was confronted with a war in which the Americans seemed to have a far better chance of victory than had ever been envisaged. The New England militiamen had Gage cooped up in Boston, and the news from the Canadian frontier could not have been more promising. There was plenty of support for reorganizing the militiamen around Boston as an inter-colonial 'Continental Army'. The biggest stumbling-block, however, was the unwillingness of the other colonial delegates to agree to the appointment of a Massachusetts officer as supreme commander. This would effectively have left Massachusetts, widely mistrusted for its cantankerous extremism, running the whole show – but the problem was brilliantly surmounted by the eventual appointment of the respected Virginian, George Washington. All this took time to be hammered out; the Continental Army was not proclaimed until 14 June, with Washington receiving his appointment on the following day. Before he could even take up his duties, the deliberations of Congress were again overtaken by dramatic events at Boston.

Inevitably out of touch with the course of events in America, the British Government sent Gage reinforcements – and orders to disperse the rebels and capture their leaders. By mid-June 1775, with about 6,000 British troops ready for action, Gage prepared to clear the decks by pushing the Americans off the heights round Boston, thus ensuring the security of the only British military foothold in the colonies. But the result was the near-disaster of 17 June 1775: the Battle of Bunker Hill, which the British took at bayonet point only after the American defenders had run out of ammunition. British casualties at Bunker Hill were appalling: 1,054 out of 2,200 with at least 226 killed. It was more than enough to force Gage back on to the defensive, pleading for massive rein-

Previous pages: The first of many triumphs for Captain John Barry of the American Continental Navy: the capture of the British sloop HMS *Edward* by the handy brigantine *Lexington* (formerly *Wild Duck*) off Cape Charles on 7 April 1776.

12

forcements which never came. Meanwhile, through the summer of 1775, Washington and his generals began to lick the Continental Army into a semblance of regular order, their sights set on an eventual move to expel the British from Boston.

As the Continental Army embarked on the siege of Boston, Congress – its hand strengthened even further by the object-lesson of Bunker Hill – was still prepared to try for a negotiated settlement with Britain. The 'Olive Branch Petition,' signed by Congress on 8 July 1775, offered no American concessions to King George. It was a protestation of unchanged colonial loyalty, coupled with a request for redress of grievances to bring about an end to hostilities. Determined never to negotiate with rebels, the King refused the Petition point-blank on 1 September: a stubborn, if hardly realistic, statement that Britain was not prepared to consider the faintest likelihood of ultimate defeat. The failure of

the 'Olive Branch Petition' left Congress with no option but to prepare for all-out war with Britain by land and sea. With its Continental Army already in the field before Boston, Congress authorized the formation of a Continental Navy on 13 October 1775.

Creating the Continental Navy was an infinitely harder task than shaping the Army, the raw formations of which were already in the field in June 1775. The biggest problem was the artillery shortage, which bedevilled American operations for the first three years of the war. With no gun foundries in the colonies, every popgun six-pounder embarked in a Navy commerce raider was one field gun less for the Army. Then again, it took time to conduct the necessary stock-taking of colonial vessels suitable for commerce raiding – and time was on the side of the British, enabling them to recommission a score of laid-up warships for every American raider sent out to prey on British commerce.

American colors fly over the British as the Continental schooner *Lee*, commanded by Captain John Manley, escorts the captured British brig *Nancy* into captivity on 28 November 1775. *Nancy*, with her cargo of gunpowder, was a prize of immense value at this early stage of the War of Independence.

An early encounter which
was typical of the hit-and-run
style of the Continental Navy.

Commodore Esek Hopkins, first commander-in-chief of the American Continental fleet. His lackluster performance contrasted ill with the more dashing successes of the American single-ship raiders and he was relieved of his command after failing to capture the British frigate HMS *Glasgow* off Block Island on 6 April 1776.

Inevitably the Continental Navy, so-called, at first consisted of a number of 'navies' raised by the different colonies. Apart from the shortage of guns, the Continental Navy suffered from an incurable dilemma. Its best privateer captains were, from the nature of such warfare, individualists, most effective when left virtually to their own devices. Congress, however, was obsessed from the start by the need to show its likeliest European allies that emergent America was far more than a mere nest of licensed pirates, hence the early attempt, late in 1775, to form a Continental 'fleet,' scraped together to make at least a show of conventional naval capacity, whose operations were always far less effective than those of individual raiders.

The fleet's commander, the first American to hold flag rank with the status of commodore, was Esek Hopkins of Rhode Island. Born in 1718 at Scituate, R.I., Hopkins had been a privateer commander in the Seven Years War and in 1775 owned a fleet of merchantmen. He was therefore qualified to command the Continental fleet on the dual grounds of previous war experience and financial self-

sufficiency, and being the younger brother of the head of the Naval Committee of Congress was no hindrance. For a flagship Hopkins was given the new merchant ship *Black Prince* of Philadelphia, hastily armed with 20 nine-pounders and 10 six-pounders and renamed *Alfred*. Her complement consisted of about 160 officers and seamen and 60 militiamen embarked as marines. 'Keeping it in the family', Hopkins' eldest son John Burroughs Hopkins commanded the brig *Cabot,* with her single deck of 14 six-pounders and 12 light swivel guns, 90 officers and seamen and 30 marines.

Apart from *Alfred,* the only other ship in the fleet with two decks of guns was *Columbus* (18 nine-pounders and 10 six-pounders). Her commander, Captain Abraham Whipple, was another Rhode Islander, born in 1733 at Providence, R.I. Getting a command in this threadbare squadron was bad luck for Whipple because he was a commerce-raiding lone wolf *par excellence*. Commanding the privateer *Gamecock* in the Seven Years War, he had captured 23 French merchantmen in six months. When hostilities against the British broke out in 1775, the Rhode Island assembly gave Whipple two ships fitted out to protect the colony's seaborne commerce. He had wasted no time in capturing the armed tender of the British frigate HMS *Rose,* the first enemy prize taken by an American warship. Though Whipple was adept at the type of naval warfare on which the Continental Navy would have to rely – hit-and-run, with maximum nuisance value – few such opportunities to shine came his way under Hopkins' command.

Captain Nicholas Biddle commanded the brig *Andrea Doria* of 16 six-pounders and 12 swivel guns, 100 officers and seamen and 30 marines. A most promising young officer, Biddle was a Pennsylvanian, born in 1750 in Philadelphia, and had gone to sea at the age of 13. Biddle was an excellent example of the fine human material suddenly denied to the Royal Navy by the breach with the American colonies, having served as a midshipman in the King's Navy in 1770. In 1773 he had requested an appointment to the Royal Society's forthcoming expedition to the North Pole, but on being refused he resigned his rank and enlisted before the mast in the bomb-ketch *Carcass*. (One of his shipmates on this abortive expedition, which returned after being halted by ice in August 1773, was the young Horatio Nelson, serving as coxswain of the captain's gig in the same spirit of adventure). When the Polar expedition returned to England in October 1773, the 'tea crisis' with the American colonies was already well advanced and Biddle returned to America. *Andrea Doria* was his first command in the service of the Pennsylvanian 'navy.'

The fifth and most junior command in the Continental fleet was Captain Hazard's light sloop *Providence,* with 12 six-pounders, ten swivel guns, 62 seamen and 28 marines. Together, the five ships of the fleet mounted 38 nine-pounders and 62 six-pounders – an extravagant concentration of guns which would have been far better employed with the Army, which in the winter of 1775-76 was preparing to batter the British out of Boston. This must be counted as a serious misapplication of the scanty resources at the disposal of Congress, which had the inevitable result of delaying the build-up of Washington's Army with no compensating gains at sea. In its anxiety to fit out a recognizable colonial fleet, Congress was forgetting that it was bound to be brutally out-gunned in any action. British frigates, the likeliest class of warship which the Colonial fleet could expect to fight, carried far heavier guns: 18-pounders, 12-pounders, on average from two to three times the weight of metal than that of the lightweight American six-pounders with their top-dressing of nine-pounders. Even a single British frigate, well handled and given the right conditions, might be expected to give a good

Below: A typically spirited encounter of the early days of the war: the capture of the British armed schooner HMS *Margaretta* off the port of Machias, Maine (11 May 1775) by 35 Patriots embarked in a lumber sloop armed with muskets, pitchforks and axes. The British captain was killed. 19 other British crewmen were killed or wounded, and the spoils included 40 cutlasses, 40 boarding axes and 40 muskets, plus grenades, pistols and two wall guns.

account of itself against Hopkins' motley armada. And so it proved.

The first mission ordered by Congress for the Continental Navy was to stop the savaging of the Virginian coast in Chesapeake Bay by the dispossessed British governor, Lord Dunmore. With a handful of light warships and a force composed of Royal Marines and negro slaves enlisted on (empty) promises of freedom, Dunmore earned the nickname of 'bloody butcher' for his raids on Virginian Patriots. Unable to maintain a base ashore, Dunmore was a menace who, if not eliminated, might conceivably tempt the British into sending a reinforcing army for the subjugation of Virginia. Dunmore's flotilla was not, in fact, an objective hopelessly beyond the capacity of the Continental fleet, but Hopkins felt otherwise. He was convinced that his ships would be far better employed in beating up the British sealanes between the American coast and the Bahamas, thus forcing the British to spread their available naval force as thinly as possible.

There was no direct collaboration between the Continental Army and the Navy's only fleet in March 1776, when the siege of Boston came to an unexpectedly early climax. On 4 March Washington occupied the commanding eminence of Dorchester Heights, emplacing heavy guns (captured at Fort Ticonderoga the previous year and painfully dragged south by sledge) to menace the city and harbor. Thus surprised, the British evacuated Boston on 17 March and shipped their garrison to Halifax, Nova Scotia. While this was going on, Hopkins and the American fleet were 1,300 miles to the south, raiding Nassau in the Bahamas. With the British fleet momentarily committed to the safe transfer of the Boston garrison to Nova Scotia, Hopkins would have been able to blockade Dunmore in Chesapeake Bay without undue molestation, but the opportunity was missed.

April 1776 came in with a symbolic pair of engagements for the Continental Navy: a humiliation for the fleet, followed within 24 hours by a brilliantly successful single-ship action.

The first event took place on 6 April: a miserable encounter between Hopkins' fleet and the British frigate HMS *Glasgow*, patrolling the mouth of Long Island Sound and the southern approaches to Rhode Island. Hopkins badly needed a solid victory, to exonerate himself to the Naval Committee for not having gone to the Chesapeake as

ordered. He had won little success at Nassau, where he had failed to capture more than a small portion of the invaluable British naval stores. Passing up an action with favorable odds of five-to-one would have crowned his failure. He had little choice but to attack *Glasgow*, but he also knew that his fleet was the only one which Congress was likely to raise, and shrank from the prospect of excessive losses. The result was an inconclusive sparring-match off Block Island from which *Glasgow* escaped with comparative ease. Though his best chance would have been a converging attack by all five American ships, culminating in boarding with overwhelming manpower, Hopkins kept the range open and tried to disable *Glasgow* with long-range sniping – over-cautious tactics ideally suited to *Glasgow*, with her heavier fire-power.

Glasgow's dry record of the encounter – the only attack ever made by an American fleet on a British warship – has survived. It is notable for its detail and the surprising extent of information which the British clearly had about the American warships (or 'Rebel Armed Vessels' as they were dismissively called). All five ships' names were known, with their captains, though *Andrea Doria* and *Cabot* are spelled as 'Annadona' and 'Cabinet.' The differing armaments and complements of the ships were also noted, with brief notes on the ships' appearances. *Alfred,* the flagship, was described as 'A Figure head and Yellow Sides, her Lower Deck Ports not above eighteen inches from the Water; Mizen Topgallant Sail.' Yellow seems to have been a Hopkins trademark, with *Cabot* described as 'A small white Figure head, and Yellow sides with hanging Ports;' *Columbus, Andrea Doria* and *Providence* were all black-painted, without figureheads.

Observers in *Glasgow* also noted that *Alfred* and *Columbus,* contrary to the normal practice of mounting light guns above heavy guns, carried their nine-pounders on the upper deck and their six-pounders below. This top-heavy arrangement, which can have done little to improve the ships' stability in a seaway, was intended to permit the nine-pounders to fire even in rough weather or during points of sailing which made it impossible to open lower-deck ports.

The humiliation of the Continental fleet off Block Island was increased when the news came through of an American single-ship victory 400 miles to the south, won on 7 April 1776. It was the first of many triumphs for

Captain John Barry, born about 1745 in County Wexford, Ireland, for whom Philadelphia had been home since 1760. He had become a merchant captain by the age of 21 and his last peacetime command had been the *Black Prince,* subsequently requisitioned as *Alfred.* Barry was commissioned as a Captain in the Continental Navy on 14 March 1776. He was appointed to command the armed brigantine *Wild Duck* which had been re-christened *Lexington,* the first of seven American warships destined to bear that illustrious name. Superbly handled by Barry, the handy *Lexington* evaded the British frigate HMS *Roebuck,* patrolling the entrance to Delaware Bay, and escaped to sea. Barry then headed south for the Chesapeake and on 7 April fell in with the British sloop HMS *Edward,* tender to the frigate HMS *Liverpool,* off Cape Charles. A communications vessel rather than a fighting ship, *Edward* had a complement of only 29 and surrendered after a running fight lasting nearly an hour – the first American prize to be brought into Philadelphia.

Though the opposition had been modest, Barry's performance had been sharply competent throughout. It was considered all the more creditable that a two-masted brigantine (with square rig on the foremast only, and fore-and-aft rig on the mainmast) had captured a nominally more powerful sloop. The lackluster performance of the Continental fleet appeared all the more depressing in the light of this timely demonstration of what could be achieved by American warships, and Esek Hopkins had to endure a vote of censure from Congress. He was given no further chance to redeem himself, being suspended from his command prior to formal dismissal. This unforgiving treatment of naval commanders who failed to fulfil the politicians' expectations was to remain a characteristic of the American naval service. Though not without value, *pour encourager les autres,* it was not invariably successful, let alone just. In the case of the Royal Navy the British often preferred to give another chance to a man who had done good service in the past, and if Hopkins had been overcautious he had at least kept the fleet in being. Whipple of the *Columbus,* incidentally, demanded a court martial to absolve himself of imputations of blame for the Block Island fiasco, and was cleared.

Such were the uncertain origins of American sea power in the first year of the War of Independence: tentative, inglorious, and yet by no means disastrous or even lacking in promise. The *Glasgow* fiasco was a sharp reminder that the Continental Navy was pitted against real professionals; the *Edward* success was a solid hint that any successes which American sailors might win would come from lucky or well-chosen encounters with opposition of suitably modest dimensions. If concentrated, vainly trying to imitate conventional fleets, the Continental Navy would be risking disaster. If dispersed in privateer commerce-raiding, it could at least continue to make an intolerable nuisance of itself. But one ugly fact was grimly obvious. Alone and unsupported, the Continental Navy had no chance of stopping the British from shipping troops anywhere they chose.

This was the hardest reality facing the American Congress as its delegates steeled themselves to sign the colonies' Declaration of Independence on 4 July 1776. At the very moment at which the American 'Founding Fathers' were signing that immortal document, British and mercenary German troops were pouring into New York, chosen as the main base from which the reconquest of the American colonies would be launched. The British build-up continued throughout July and August 1776 and by early autumn the Continental Army was confronted by about 45,000 British and German troops, 10,000 of them in Canada and the rest massed in New York. In the face of this massive new development, the only discernible American naval success was the capture of three armed transports on 16-17 June. This was achieved by Captain Seth Harding of Massachusetts in the brig *Defence,* fitted out by the Connecticut State Navy – a pinprick against an elephant.

The summer and early autumn of 1776 saw the British complete their ominous new troop concentration in New York, with the Continental Navy completely unable to stop or even delay it. Extreme measures were called for, and none was more extreme than the attempt to blow up the British naval C-in-C, Admiral Howe, in his flagship. This took place in August 1776 and, though a failure, was an historic event: the first attack by a submersible craft with an explosive warhead. The 'submarine' in question was the brain-child of David Bushnell, who had graduated from Yale in 1775. Bushnell's *Turtle* was a wooden egg enclosing a single crewman and hand-pumped buoyancy tanks by which the craft could be 'trimmed down'

U.S.S. "TURTLE" 1776

just below the surface. Feeble power was provided by hand-cranked screws, and *Turtle* was also fitted with a vertical gimlet for screwing into the bottom planking of the target ship. To this gimlet was attached an explosive charge, to be left beneath the target as *Turtle* made its escape.

The *Turtle* attack was not, however, a Navy affair: it was carried out by Sergeant Ezra Lee of the Continental Army, against Howe's flagship HMS *Eagle,* lying in the lower East River. It was a gallant effort deserving of better success. Lee did extraordinarily well to fetch up under *Eagle's* stern after a downstream approach, but he was beaten by a new British 'secret weapon' for which *Turtle's* designer had not bargained: the new technique of protecting ships' hulls with copper sheathing. This defeated all Lee's efforts to force home *Tur-*

tle's gimlet and in the end he was forced to beat a retreat, chased by boats from *Eagle*. Lee managed to escape them by slipping the explosive charge and detonating it in the face of his pursuers.

The *Turtle* incident is usually remembered as an untimely freak of naval history, but it has more significance than that. In its audacity alone, it perfectly demonstrated American desperation in the face of a relentless British amphibious build-up against which available American naval resources were useless. As a might-have-been – Lee came close to success – it is on a par with wondering what would have happened if Hitler had not declared war on the United States when the Japanese attacked Pearl Harbor in December 1941. If Lee *had* succeeded in blowing one of Britain's most respected admirals sky-high it would have

The first 'submarine attack' in naval history: Ezra Lee's gallant but unavailing foray against HMS *Eagle*, flagship of the British Admiral Howe, in the East River on 7 September 1776.

E. TUFNELL

been remembered as an atrocity, a renunciation of the rules of civilized warfare; and one of the biggest paradoxes of the War of Independence was that the British fought it very much according to the rules of civilized warfare. Though the British officially regarded the war, from start to finish, as the suppression of rebellion, captured American captains were not hanged or shot as rebels. They were offered the same niceties expected by any European belligerent of the day: release on parole, or imprisonment pending exchange for a captured British officer of equivalent rank.

Under this polite system, many American officers underwent more than one spell of British captivity before either escaping or being exchanged, returning to sea to fight the British again. They included John Barry, Gustavus Conyngham, Richard Dale, John Manley, and Samuel Tucker. A harder British line towards prisoners of war could easily have resulted from a successful attack by *Turtle,* progressively depriving the struggling Congress of its best seagoing commanders.

American fortunes reached a nadir in the autumn and winter of 1776-77, with Washington's army successively pushed out of Long Island, away from New York and

The Stars and Stripes in the English Channel: USS *Revenge*, commanded by the aggressive commerce raider Captain Gustavus Conyngham (1777-1778).

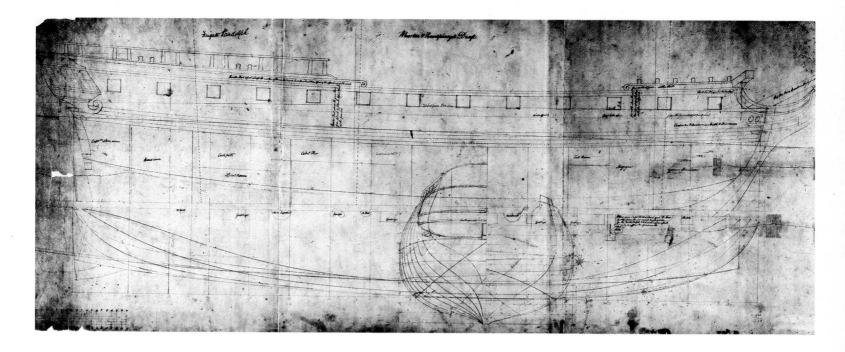

across New Jersey into Pennsylvania. Across the Atlantic, however, French sympathy for the American cause burgeoned under the subtle hand of envoy Benjamin Franklin, who arrived in Paris in December 1776. Though the French held back from a formal alliance until February 1778, Franklin did win permission for American raiders to refit and operate from French ports. One of his first achievements was to secure the release of Gustavus Conyngham, jailed by the French for operating out of Dunkirk in the lugger *Surprise* and bringing his prizes into French ports. Conyngham, another Irish-born Philadelphian, had learned navigation in his cousin's merchant ship, and had been stranded in Europe when the war broke out in 1775. The first American raider to carry the naval war into British waters, Conyngham was commissioned Captain in the Continental Navy by Franklin. He made a successful raiding cruise in the North and Irish Seas in the cutter *Revenge* before shifting to Spanish ports when France and Spain entered the war. By the time Conyngham returned to Philadelphia via the West Indies in February 1779 he had taken 60 prizes in 18 months.

The year 1777 was the turning-point of the war, seeing General Sir William Howe fail to destroy Washington's army and switching his objective to capturing Philadelphia. British sea power enabled Howe to shift his army from New York to Chesapeake Bay, but this move left General Burgoyne unsupported as he began what was intended to be a decisive southward march from Canada. The result was not the planned British isolation and reconquest of New England by the united armies of Burgoyne and Howe, but the isolation of Burgoyne's army and its surren-

der at Saratoga on 17 October 1777. This triumph more than atoned for the loss of Philadelphia to Howe in late September, and the discomfiture of Washington's army at Valley Forge in the winter of 1777-78. The most important direct result of Saratoga was the signing of treaties of commerce and alliance on 6 February 1778 between France and the newly-styled 'United States of America.' Assuming, after Saratoga, that there was no longer any danger of the American colonies falling to converging attack, the alliance guaranteed them the aid of the French battle fleet and the eventual despatch (July 1780) of a French expeditionary force to fight alongside the Continental Army.

Thanks to Franklin's advocacy, however, the first fruits of the alliance were gathered even before the treaties were signed. French co-operation in the naval war saw the step-ping-up of American activity in British home waters, and an increased flow of military and naval supplies from France to America. These vital facilities saved the United States from the humiliation of having to entrust the naval war entirely to the French fleet. In 1777-78 it enabled the fitting-out of a new generation of American warships, the light frigates *Randolph*, *Warren*, *Hancock*, *Confederacy* and *Boston*, the first of which were ready for sea in the early summer of 1777.

The new raiders scored an early success, but this was cancelled almost at once. In June 1777, with *Boston* in company, John Manley in *Hancock* captured the British light frigate HMS *Fox*. Manley continued his cruise with *Fox* under an American prize crew, but within a month of this cheering victory he had the bad luck to fall in with two British frigates and a brig detached to hunt him down. With his manpower spread too

The only surviving plan drawn for one of the new frigates of the Continental Navy: USS *Randolph*, built at Philadelphia in 1776 to the design of Wharton and Humphries. Sadly, *Randolph's* service career was brief: she blew up in action with the British 64-gun *Yarmouth* in March 1778, near Barbados.

American frigates *Boston* and *Hancock* in action against the British *Flora* and *Rainbow* off Cape Sable, Newfoundland (7 July 1777).

thinly between *Hancock* and *Fox,* Manley was forced to strike his colors while *Fox* was speedily recaptured. Manley was exchanged after a year in British captivity and returned to face an American court-martial for losing *Hancock*. He was acquitted, and returned to sea with more successes in store for him.

By this time, however, the Continental Navy had lost not only the second of its new frigates, but one of its most promising captains. Biddle, formerly commanding *Andrea Doria* under Esek Hopkins, was fifth in the captains' list by the New Year of 1778 and promoted to the new *Randolph*. In March

Block Island fiasco against *Glasgow,* and at first *Randolph,* excellently handled, stood up well to *Yarmouth's* greatly superior fire-power. But it ended disastrously when *Randolph* blew up – a most unusual end to a single-ship duel, indicative of inadequate magazine protection – with Biddle among the many dead.

The tragic loss of Biddle and *Randolph* in March 1778 was rapidly followed by the first exploits of one of the most celebrated of all American naval heroes: John Paul Jones. Born in 1747 at Kirkbean, Galloway, he was the son of an Irish gardener named John Paul, and, bearing the same name, first went to sea in the British merchant service in 1761. At Tobago in 1773, John Paul killed a mutinous seaman. This was in self-defense but he still had to flee to Virginia, where his elder brother was a tailor, taking the name 'Jones' in the process. After service as a lieutenant in the Continental Navy, Jones got his first command, the new sloop *Ranger,* in 1777. His first task was to supervize

Captain John Paul Jones and *(below)* a recruiting poster soliciting recruitment of 'gentlemen volunteers' for his first command, the new sloop *Ranger,* in March 1777.

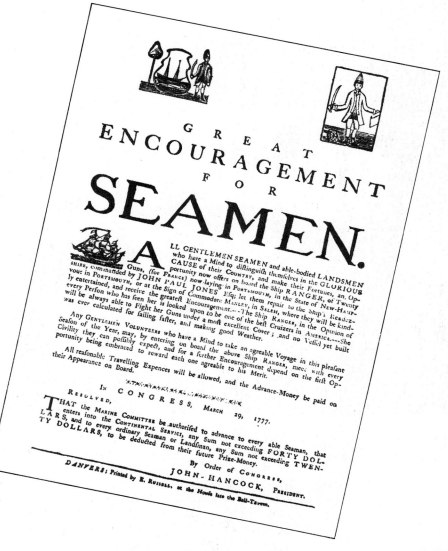

1778, having sailed from Charleston with four light warships of the South Carolina State Navy in company, Biddle in *Randolph* fell in with the British 64-gun HMS *Yarmouth* near Barbados, and boldly engaged this much stronger adversary. It was an obvious bid to wipe out the shame of the

Ranger's completion and fitting-out at Portsmouth, New Hampshire, before sailing for France, arriving at Nantes on 2 December.

When he met Franklin in Paris, Jones learned that *Ranger's* arrival could not have been more timely. It coincided with that of confirmatory news of the British capitulation at Saratoga and the acceleration of Franco-American alliance talks. As the most convincing demonstration of the American will to carry the war to the British enemy, Franklin ordered Jones to raid in British home waters in the spring of 1778. This was preceded on 14 February by the first-ever formal salute of a ship flying the 'Stars and Stripes' by warships of a foreign power, rendered to *Ranger* in Quiberon Bay.

Ranger's cruise of March-May 1778 began with an abortive night raid on the Cumbrian port of Whitehaven during 22-23 April. This caused little material damage, but the moral effect of American raiders landing on British soil was naturally immense. On the following day, Jones raided the home of the Earl of Selkirk at St Mary's, planning to take the Earl as a hostage for a mass release of American prisoners of war. Unfortunately the Earl was not at home. The raiders made off with his family silver instead, but Jones subsequently demonstrated his hold over his men by returning the silver with a note of apology.

The highlight of the cruise came on 24 April when *Ranger,* approaching Belfast Lough, encountered the British sloop HMS *Drake.* It was one of the most equally-matched single-ship actions of the war and Jones fought it brilliantly, concentrating on cutting his opponent's rigging to pieces with disabling fire. Finally, when the British commander had been killed, the master of *Drake* surrendered. Jones crowned his vic-

The first 'famous victory' for John Paul Jones, 24 April 1778. At left the British sloop HMS *Drake*, her rigging already showing the effects of American disabling shot, trails her shattered bowsprit overside at the outset of the action off Belfast which ended in her capture.

Woodcut of the 32-gun American frigate *Alliance*, commanded by the unreliable French expatriate Pierre Landais during the epic cruise of John Paul Jones in *Bonhomme Richard*.

tory by fitting *Drake* with a jury rig and bringing her triumphantly into Brest – an additional humiliation for the Royal Navy in home waters, on a par with the successful running of the English Channel by the German warships *Scharnhorst* and *Gneisenau* in February 1942. From France, 200 British prisoners were subsequently exchanged for American prisoners in British hands. Deeply impressed by Jones's achievement, the French agreed to contribute warships to a Franco-American squadron to be commanded by Jones on a second cruise in 1779.

As the French authorities had all they could do to render their battle fleet fit for action in American waters, Jones got the scrapings. His 'flagship' was the old French East Indiaman *Duc de Duras*, renamed *Bonhomme Richard*. She took a year to fit out at Lorient, modified to carry the motley armament of six 18-pounders, 28 12-pounders and eight nine-pounders. Jones was also given the 30-gun *Pallas* and 12-gun *Vengeance* – both armed merchantmen – and the 18-gun cutter *Cerf*. The American contribution to the squadron was the new Continental frigate *Alliance*, of 32 guns. As her name implied, she was a reciprocal compliment to the Franco-American alignment and, to the disappointment of many better-qualified American officers, was commanded by a Frenchman. He was Pierre Landais, a French naval officer who had gone to fight for the American Patriots in 1777 and had been commissioned into the Continental Navy. His undoubted propaganda value could not, as it proved, atone for his erratic and unstable behaviour in command. Landais brought *Alliance* into Brest in February 1779, but it was June before Jones had his squadron fit for sea. When it sailed, on 19 June, *Bonhomme Richard* and *Alliance* collided heavily and the need for repairs meant a further delay until 14 August.

Safely to sea at last, Jones pressed ahead with his planned circumnavigation of the British Isles, despite the weakening of his force by the incompetence and wilfulness of his junior commanders. The cutter *Cerf* lost touch with the squadron off south-west Ireland, and never rejoined; Landais in *Alliance* kept taking off on what appeared to be his private commerce-raiding war. Thanks to Landais's refusal to co-operate, Jones had to abandon his intended entry of the Firth of Forth to raise Cain off the Scottish capital of Edinburgh. But the squadron's fortunes improved on the voyage down the English east coast, with three prizes snapped up off Flamborough Head on 21 September, and Jones remained in what seemed a promising hunting-ground. He was right. On the 23rd, the ideal target hove into view: a 41-ship convoy from the Baltic, scantily escorted by the 20-gun *Countess of Scarborough* and the 44-gun frigate *Serapis*, commanded by Captain Richard Pearson.

There was no choice but to fight, as Pearson stoutly positioned *Serapis* and *Countess of Scarborough* between this unex-

Robert Dodd's painting of the famous duel between John Paul Jones in *Bonhomme Richard* (at centre left) and HMS *Serapis* off Flamborough Head (23 September 1779). *Alliance*, firing indiscriminately into both friend and foe, is shown circling the main action at right, with the secondary duel between the American *Pallas* and HMS *Countess of Scarborough* at left.

pected enemy force and the helpless merchantmen of the convoy. Jones duly headed in to take out *Serapis,* reckoning that this would be straightforward enough with *Alliance* in support; but he was again let down, with near-fatal consequences, by the maddening behaviour of Landais. In the ensuing epic Battle of Flamborough Head, *Pallas* battered the weaker *Countess of Scarborough* while *Bonhomme Richard* and *Serapis* fought it out, with Landais in *Alliance* circling the fray and firing into both friend and foe alike.

In the duel between *Bonhomme Richard* and *Serapis,* British gunnery and seamanship told from the first. Pearson managed to rake *Bonhomme Richard,* two of whose 18-pounders burst at the beginning of the action. *Bonhomme Richard* took a fearful battering for two hours, at the end of which she was leaking like a sieve (kept afloat largely by the efforts of the prisoners of war turned loose by Jones to labor at the pumps) with only three nine-pounders still able to fire. Pearson then called on Jones to surrender – as did several of Jones's own men – only to receive the immortal defiance, 'I have not yet begun to fight!' Jones made good his words by laying *Bonhomme Richard* alongside *Serapis* and boarding: the only option left to him. *Serapis* was carried against stiff resistance, which only wilted when Landais belatedly closed and opened a devastating raking fire. At 10.30pm, knowing that he had saved his convoy and that his men could do no more, Pearson surrendered to Jones – whose first act was to transfer his men from the foundering *Bonhomme Richard* to *Serapis.*

It had been a bloody encounter, with 128 killed and wounded in *Serapis* and 150 in *Bonhomme Richard.* Jones painfully crossed the North Sea to the Texel and the temporary shelter of Dutch neutrality. There, now flying his commodore's broad pendant in *Alliance,* he managed to repair *Serapis* before sailing again on 27 December. On 19 February 1780, after evading the British squadrons hunting for him and making a cruise across the Bay of Biscay to Corunna, Jones reached Lorient. In Holland Jones had been joined by Gustavus Conyngham, who had been captured off New York earlier in the year and imprisoned in England before escaping with the help of friends in London. (Conyngham returned to America from Corunna only to be captured again, this time spending a year in prison before being re-

leased under exchange.) Meanwhile, back in Paris, Jones revelled in a well-earned hero's welcome before returning to America in the sloop *Ariel.* Congress appointed him to complete and command the Continental Navy's first battleship, the 74-gun *America,* under construction at Portsmouth, New Hampshire.

Though naturally high in propaganda value and dramatic impact, the exploits of Conyngham and Jones in British home waters had no direct effect on the course of the war in America. The spring of 1778 had seen Washington's army speedily restored from the hardships of the winter, improved by European drill, and able to take the field. The British in Philadelphia, unable to destroy Washington, were now faced with imminent French intervention; Philadelphia was therefore abandoned to permit a concentration at New York. In July 1778 the Comte d'Estaing arrived off the Delaware Capes with a battle fleet 11 strong. When he moved to New York Admiral Howe, momentarily outnumbered, kept his ships close inshore to cover the British garrison, but d'Estaing failed to combine with Washington in a joint attack on the city. The moment of danger passed with d'Estaing's removal, first to support an abortive siege of Newport, Rhode Island, and then in August 1778 to Boston. The British were not slow to profit from d'Estaing's hesitation. At the end of 1778 they took the offensive again, sending forces from New York to occupy French St Lucia in the Caribbean and Savannah in Georgia.

Apart from New York, the British had effectively cut their losses in the north and it was in the Southern States – Georgia (1778-79), the Carolinas (1779-80) and Virginia (1781) – that the war was fought to its conclusion. Apart from fleeting successes in the field, the last solid British success was the capture of Charleston on 12 May 1780, together with a squadron of four American warships (*Providence, Ranger, Queen of France* and *Boston*) trying to emulate Howe's defense of New York in 1778. The senior American naval officer at Charleston was Abraham Whipple, deploring this misuse of the Continental Navy's still-modest resources. Only one year previously, Whipple in *Providence,* with two auxiliaries, had got in among a British homebound convoy and captured ten of its ships before the escorting British warships could react. But Charleston was the last major American naval setback of the war, which was effectively won by the

The decisive fleet action of the War of Independence (5 September 1781) ended with the defeat of the British battle fleet under Admiral Graves (*right*) by the French under the Comte de Grasse.

Comte de Grasse's defeat of Admiral Graves's fleet at the entrance to Chesapeake Bay on 5 September 1781. This crucial defeat left General Cornwallis's army isolated on Virginia's Yorktown peninsula, with the French fleet to seaward and the Franco-American army to landward. Cornwallis bowed to the inevitable and surrendered on 19 October 1781.

It was clear to all that Britain had no hope of regaining her former American colonies by force, being now at war not only with France but with Spain (from June 1779) and the Dutch Republic (from December 1780). During the two years which separated the Yorktown surrender from the signing of the definitive Peace of Paris on 3 September 1783, American privateers and ships of the Continental Navy kept up the attack on

British commerce. The last important prize of the war was the merchant ship *Baille,* captured by John Manley in the Continental frigate *Hague* in January 1783. Two months later came the last clash with the Royal Navy. In March 1783, escorting a bullion ship carrying 72,000 dollars, John Barry in *Alliance* fought the British frigate HMS *Sybil,* brought down her foretopmast with his first broadside, and drove her off after 40 minutes. This action, in its sharp competence, was reminiscent of the skill with which Barry had extricated *Alliance* from attack by HMS *Atlanta* and *Trepassy* two years before.

The Continental Navy's contribution to American victory was always secondary: the commerce-raiding campaign, in which it accounted for about 200 British ships. American privateering, however, had always been far more popular and profitable than service with the Navy of Congress. It has been estimated that at the time of Yorktown in

1781 there were more Americans involved in privateering than there were serving in Washington's army. American privateers took nearly four British ships for every one which fell to the Continental Navy, estimates of the joint tally ranging from 800 to 1,000 vessels. A contemporary English estimate put the financial loss to the British war effort caused by American raiders at some £2 million.

Faced with swarming political, constitutional and financial problems of the utmost urgency, Congress had no intention whatever of maintaining a peacetime fleet of any kind. It took the States until April 1789 to agree on a joint constitution and swear in Washington as first President of the United States, and until this had been done Congress had no authority to levy taxes for such costly peacetime expenditure. Indeed, Congress began selling off ships of the Continental fleet long before the Peace of Paris was signed. The new '74', *America,* went to

The British frigate HMS *Mediator* (*left*) surprised by the French ships *Menagère, Eugène* and *Dauphin Royal* and the American *Alexander* with an American brig on 12 December 1782.

France in 1782, thus abruptly and ungratefully ending the career of John Paul Jones in American service. (He died of pneumonia in Paris ten years later, having briefly served as a rear-admiral in the Russian Navy of Catherine the Great). By the time of the Peace of Paris Barry's *Alliance* was the last warship left flying the American flag, and she was sold in 1785. For the Continental Navy, the price of American victory in the War of Independence was immediate dissolution, in the vague hope that friendly powers would in future give the United States any naval protection that might be needed.

It took little over ten years for the American Republic to accept hard reality: that the United States' essential seaborne trade would remain vulnerable as long as naval protection was lacking. From the middle 1780s, attacks on American merchant shipping by corsairs from Algiers and Tripoli — international pests swarming inside and outside the Mediterranean — left the United States with no choice but to pay the corsairs protection-money, or leave American merchantmen to their fate. Nor, when Europe became involved in war against Revolutionary France in 1792-93, was it feasible for American seaborne trade in the Mediterranean to claim the already-dubious protection of European navies. American refusal to become involved in the European conflict, signified by Washington's proclamation of neutrality in April 1793, only spelled out the fact that the American merchant marine was overdue for at least a token measure of American naval protection.

On 27 March 1794, a special Act of Congress provided for the formation of the United States Navy. Admittedly, 'navy' could be described as a grandiose term for the six frigates provided for in the Act, but there was a vital difference from the hodge-podge nature of the old Continental Navy. The new United States Navy was to be nationally funded, with an initial appropriation of two-thirds of a million dollars, not scraped together from the contributions of the individual states.

Bringing the 'original six frigates' from approval on paper into reality could well be called Washington's last great service to his country. He picked the captains who would oversee completion of the new ships — respected veterans from the War of Independence, men like John Barry, Richard Dale,

Thomas Truxton. Most important of all, it was Washington who appointed the remarkable naval designer Joshua Humphreys, a supreme pragmatist who realized that the new frigates must be able to out-sail and out-gun all contemporary ships of their class. As Humphreys put it, 'As our navy for a considerable time will be inferior in numbers, we are to consider what size ships will be most formidable and be an overmatch for those of an enemy.' Humphreys opted for 'qualities of strength, durability, swiftness of sailing and force — superior to any frigate.'

Thanks to Washington and Humphreys, the 'original six frigates' of the United States Navy — *Constellation, Constitution, Congress, Chesapeake, United States,* and *President* — were the pocket-battleships of the age of sail. Their completion was supervised by the specially-formed Department of the Navy, created with the US Marine Corps on 30 April 1798. It was none too soon. By June 1798, the United States was already involved in its first naval war.

Captain John Barry, senior captain of the new US Navy (by virtue of his services in the War of Independence) when the new service was formed by Act of Congress in March 1794.

2: SURVIVAL AND TRIUMPH 1798-1823

It was certainly an irony of history that the first war which the United States had to fight was against France, the erstwhile liberator of the American colonies, but the Revolutionary France of the 1790s was a very different power from the Bourbon France of the 1770s. Luckily, the Franco-American confrontation resulted in the only form of warfare which the United States was able to wage, and no conflict could have done more to justify and expand the new United States Navy. It lasted from 1797 to 1800 and luckily for the United States was a purely naval struggle, sporadic and low key. An outright declaration of war between France and the United States was never in fact made, and hostilities took the form of mutual harrassment at sea.

The root cause of this war was French resentment and distrust not only of American neutrality, but of the successful resolution of Anglo-American frontier and trade disagreements outstanding from the Peace of Paris. These disagreements were momentarily resolved by Jay's Treaty, negotiated in London by John Jay and signed on 19 November 1794. The Revolutionary French Directory which followed Robespierre's Terror in 1795 took Jay's Treaty as a sign that the United States had become a British client in an act of 'hostile neutrality.' The Directory refused to receive Charles Pinckney as American minister in December 1796, and when he was summoned to Paris in October 1797 to smooth over the differences between France and the United States it was to receive unashamed French demands for cash payments to secure peace – nothing less than protection-money if paid. Pinckney indignantly rejected these demands while John Adams, Washington's successor as President, reaped political kudos by publishing details of the affair (the 'XYZ Affair', as it is known, 'X', 'Y' and 'Z' referring to the three French agents involved).

These events determined the diplomatic rupture between France and the United States, but a campaign of intimidation at the expense of American shipping had already begun, with several American merchant ships falling prey to French raiders by the summer of 1797. The United States Navy was in no condition to retaliate until the first of the new frigates were ready for sea in the following year. Naturally the greatest support for the Navy came from the big merchant seaports, whose prosperity was most at risk; one of the most-resented French outrages was the destruction by a French privateer of a British merchantman in Charleston Harbour. Several seaports raised funds to build warships which were then loaned indefinitely to the Navy. The most valuable of these were light frigates with broadsides about 10-15 guns lighter than those of the 'original six'. A typical example was the 36-gun *Essex,* funded by and built at Salem, Massachusetts, between April and September 1799. Pennsylvania's *Philadelphia* was another. Other seaports fitted out lighter warships, sloops, brigs and schooners, as tenders and scouts for the frigates.

As long as the conflict dragged on, the main American defensive measure was the convoying of merchant ships. As soon as *Essex* was completed and handed over to the US Navy in December 1799 she was ordered to make a maiden cruise to Batavia, Java, thence to escort home a rich convoy from the Far East trade. *Congress,* one of the 'original six', was to have gone with *Essex,* but had to turn back for repairs. This left *Essex* to become the first US warship to double the Cape of Good Hope. Her Captain, Edward Preble, had been born at Falmouth (then New Hampshire) in 1761, and had first gone to sea at the age of 16 in a privateer. In 1779 he had transferred to the Massachusetts State Navy as a midshipman. Captured in the *Proctor* in 1781, Preble was subsequently exchanged, ended the war in the Massachusetts frigate *Winthrop,* then returned to civilian life and 15 years in the merchant service. Preble's success in single-handedly bringing home the Batavia convoy in November 1800 made him a man of mark in the US Navy.

Before the undeclared Franco-American war was ended by the Treaty of Mortfontaine in September 1800, France and the United States lost about 100 merchant ships apiece in three years of sporadic raiding and retaliation. The outstanding American achievement during the conflict was the first battle fought by one of the 'original six' frigates, when the Baltimore-built *Constellation* fought and captured the French frigate *l'Insurgente* on 9 February 1799. Born at Jamaica, Long Island in 1755, Captain Thomas Truxton of *Constellation* had gone to sea at the age of 12 and in 1771 had been impressed into the Royal Navy, briefly serving in HMS *Prudent.* Truxton had been a successful privateer commander in the War of Independence, returning to the merchant service and voyaging as far afield as China

Previous page: The beginning of the end for the British frigate HMS *Macedonian* in her duel with USS *United States* (25 October 1812). *Macedonian*'s mizzenmast can already be seen floating in the sea to the right of the picture. By the end of the one-sided action the British frigate had been battered to a wreck.

before being selected for the US Navy in 1794. After his triumph over *l'Insurgente,* Truxton fought a second single-ship action in February 1800: a night encounter with *la Vengeance* of 40 guns, slightly greater than the broadside of *Constellation.* This time, however, Truxton's luck was out: he was robbed of a second victory by *Constellation's* mainmast going over the side, but emerged safely with enhanced credit from this encounter with a ship of superior force.

The foremost younger officer to make his name in the 'quasi-war' with France was Lieutenant Charles Stewart, born at Philadelphia in 1778. After first going to sea as a cabin-boy in the merchant service, Stewart was commissioned lieutenant in the US Navy in 1798, his first ship being John Barry's frigate *United States.* Here Stewart shone to such good effect that in January 1800, aged 22, he was given command of the armed schooner *Experiment.* In her, Stewart not only captured two armed French merchantmen but recaptured several American ships which had fallen victim to the French raiders. It was a brilliant beginning to a unique career in the US Navy.

In contrast to these successes, *Constitution,* destined to become the most famous of all the 'original six' frigates, had a frustrating debut in the 'quasi-war'. Of the two prizes she took, one turned out to be a British ship, while the second proved to be a British ship recently captured by the French. Because of the overriding need to preserve American neutrality in the Anglo-French conflict, *Con-*

The spirited single-ship duel between Captain Thomas Truxton in USS *Constellation (right)* and the French frigate *Vengeance* (1 February 1800). Truxton was robbed of victory by the untimely loss of *Constellation's* mainmast, but emerged with credit from the encounter.

Prize crew away: the men of USS *Enterprise* prepare to board the battered Corsair *Tripoli* – only to be forced to release their prey under the complex niceties of international law which bedevilled the US Navy during its struggle with the Barbary Corsairs (1801-1805).

stitution was robbed of her prey, her crew suffering the mortification of having to turn a prize loose and watch it sail off under the enemy's colours.

On balance, the US Navy had stood up well to its first trial, against the commerce-raiders of a major European sea power with the bulk of its navy tied down in a major European war. It was perhaps inevitable that the next exercise of sea power by President and Congress falsely sought to apply the experiences of the Franco-American 'quasi-war' to an entirely different set of circumstances.

The problem was the old one of the Barbary Corsairs in the Mediterranean, or more accurately the easternmost nest of them: Tripoli. In May 1801 the Pasha of Tripoli, discontented with the takings of peacetime extortion, decided to boost his profits from American shipping by going to war with the United States, barely three months after the third President, Thomas Jefferson, had taken office. Jefferson's options were strictly limited. The rough-hewn American Constitution prevented him from committing the United States to war. He could send a squadron to the Mediterranean in defence of American shipping, but only with a strictly defensive brief. American warships could defend themselves and any other American vessel from attack, but could not take Tripolitan prizes, destroy Tripolitan shipping or bombard Tripolitan property, let alone Tripoli itself. The most promising bloodless way of putting pressure on Tripoli seemed to be by blockade – but without injuring the trade of Tripoli's Corsair neighbours – Tunis, Algiers and Morocco, which was impossible.

From 4,000 miles away, however, it was easy for politicians to imagine that the softest option of blockade would, after less than a year's application, end with the Pasha suing for peace on American terms. It was only after the first American squadron arrived in the Mediterranean that the men on the spot found out the hard way that any blockade of Tripoli was bound to leak like a sieve, and that more forceful measures were essential.

Command of the expedition was to have gone to Truxton after his prowess in the 'quasi-war' against France, but he turned it down in a fit of pique caused by a disagreement over the appointment of his flag captain. It passed to Captain Richard Dale, onetime first lieutenant to Jones in *Bonhomme Richard,* and justly famed in the US Navy as having been the first man into *Serapis* during the Flamborough Head battle. Dale, a Virginian from Norfolk County, was 45 years old in 1801. His command consisted of the big frigate *President,* light frigates *Essex* and *Philadelphia,* and the schooner *Enterprise.* They sailed for the Mediterranean in June 1801.

The American squadron arrived at Gibraltar in July, and at once it seemed that all the confidence had been justified. Dale's force found two Tripolitan raiders – one-third of the estimated Tripolitan fleet – making ready in Gibraltar for their next foray into the Atlantic. Dale politely informed the Tripolitan commander that he would sail only at his peril, then left *Philadelphia* to stand over the cornered raiders. When the Tripolitan crews ran out of supplies they abandoned their ships, leaving them to swing round their anchors in British custody while the Tripolitans took to the boats and headed for the North African shore across the Straits.

This was exactly the sort of bloodless happy ending for which Jefferson and his advisers had hoped, but it proved to be the last of its kind. Dale headed east towards Tripoli, looking in at Algiers and Tunis to make a polite show of force, but was then obliged to detach *Essex* on convoy escort duty and *Enterprise* to replenish water supplies at Malta.

President's arrival off Tripoli certainly made a powerful impression, and Tripolitan seaborne traffic ceased as long as she remained; but this impression swiftly evaporated when Dale, after two and a half weeks' patrolling, also ran short of water and headed for Malta. The American naval presence seemed even flimsier to the Pasha when, before the week was out, the extremely battered *Tripoli* returned to her home port. *Tripoli* had had the bad luck to fall in with *Enterprise* while the latter was still on her way to Malta, and had been captured without the loss of a single American life. But then the American commander, well aware of the constitutional shackles clamped round his country's belligerency, had turned *Tripoli* loose without taking prisoners, hostages or even loot. So far from being the hoped-for show of strength, *Tripoli's* capture and release had precisely the opposite effect. The Tripolitan Corsairs had never met an enemy like this – amateur, weak, and apparently plain stupid as far as the waging of war at sea was concerned. After the *Tripoli* incident,

Dale's hopes of negotiating from a show of strength never stood a chance, and he soon made matters worse. On his way back to Tripoli from Malta, *President* stopped a Greek ship bound for Tripoli, took off 40 Tripolitans found aboard (20 of them soldiers), then landed these prisoners at Tripoli on the verbal assurance that American captives would be released in exchange. Apart from the fact that such false assurances had been a Corsair stock-in-trade for centuries, there were no American prisoners in Tripoli at the time.

Dale stuck to his thankless task for as long as he could, from September 1801 to February 1802, but with two frigates always on convoy escort duty and one ship always in transit to replenish at Malta, this left only one ship to keep an intermittent watch on Tripoli. Moreover, by the New Year of 1802, Dale was being bombarded with unhelpful advice from the American consuls in Tunis, Algiers and Morocco, warning that the other Corsair states were preparing to raise the ante – not only with increased cash demands, but with raiders already being fitted out. Dale finally headed for home in *President* in February 1802 with his crew's commission

left with barely two months to run; the fact that the squadron's sailors had only been recruited for one year's service was the most telling proof that the problem of bringing Tripoli to heel had been grossly underestimated.

Much had been learned about the practical side of that problem, however, and Jefferson's Government prepared for a second try – this time with a stronger squadron, recruited for long-term service. With *Essex, Philadelphia* and *Enterprise* as the foundation, remaining in the Mediterranean after Dale's departure, it was hoped that no less than 12 American warships could be concentrated there. But, although Congress had empowered the President to declare war on avowed enemies of the Union, the new commodore, Captain Richard Morris, was still under orders to negotiate from strength rather than fight. He was authorized to offer up to $20,000 in securing a lasting settlement with the Corsairs.

Morris's squadron, based on the big frigates *Chesapeake* and *Constellation,* with the light frigates *New York, Boston* and *John Adams,* arrived in Gibraltar in June 1802. There the first task was to repair *Che-*

Another Tripolitan Corsair falls victim to the American armed schooner *Enterprise (left)* during the war with Tripoli.

sapeake's mainmast, which had split on the Atlantic crossing. At once, Morris was plunged into the morass of problems which had bedevilled his predecessor. With Morocco now peremptorily demanding the two Tripolitan ships at Gibraltar and threatening war, Morris lacked the ships with which to watch Morocco, convoy warships and settle accounts with Tripoli.

It was now clear that only a close blockade of Tripoli would bring the Pasha to heel, but this was impossible without the shallow-draught warships (brigs and schooners) which alone could venture close inshore amid the treacherous shoals outside the port. Though *Chesapeake's* mainmast had been repaired, her bowsprit had been found to be rotten, necessitating more lengthy repairs at Malta. *New York* was badly damaged by an accidental powder explosion. The squadron's manpower constantly dropped towards danger level, due to the need to keep sending home men whose enlistments had expired. The independently-minded Captain McNeill

of *Boston* remained out of touch for weeks on end. To cap it all, Congress baulked at the cost of the expedition and insisted on the recall of *Constellation* and *Chesapeake*. Morris was a dogged, honest officer of no more than average competence, when it needed a genius to overcome the problems surrounding him at every turn.

The only highlights of the cruise were provided by Captain John Rodgers of *John Adams,* born in 1773 in Harford County, Maryland. Rodgers had been Truxton's executive officer in *Constellation* in 1799 and had been appointed prize commander of the captured *l'Insurgente*. In *John Adams,* Rodgers took the first prize achieved during the cruise: the former Tripolitan raider *Meshuda,* which in the spring of 1803 made a run for Tripoli crammed with Moroccan stores. *Meshuda* was in fact American in origin – the *Betsey* of Boston, taken by the Corsairs back in 1784 – and her recapture naturally boosted American morale. But Morris failed to follow up this success. An abortive attack

by *New York*, *John Adams* and *Enterprise* failed to prevent a shallow-draught convoy of grain ships from reaching Tripoli protected by gunboats, and a half-hearted attack on the gunboats in Tripoli harbour was also beaten off. Morris then tried negotiation, offering $5,000 for a settlement with Tripoli (he had to keep back the other $15,000 to settle with Morocco, Algiers and Tunis) but this only produced a contemptuous counter-demand for the impossible sum of $200,000 in cash, plus compensation in full for Tripoli's costs in the war.

After this humiliating rebuff Morris sailed for Malta, leaving Rodgers to maintain the blockade of Tripoli with *Enterprise* and *John Adams*. In June 1803, with a brilliant display of ship-handling, Rodgers fought and blew up a Tripolitan blockade-runner in sight of the Tripolitan army, but Morris did not exploit this success by renewing pressure on Tripoli harbour. Instead he raised the blockade and sailed for Gibraltar, only to encounter official notification of his recall. A

court of enquiry ruled that Morris be dismissed from the service – a grossly unfair sentence, with Morris denied the right to defend himself in a proper court martial. But though Morris had been cast in the role of scapegoat, Jefferson and Secretary of the Navy Robert Smith were determined to fight on, accepting the futility of the half-measures enjoined upon both Dale and Morris. Congress had also been persuaded to vote $96,000 to fit out the light warships required to close the stranglehold on Tripoli: the schooners *Nautilus* and *Vixen*, and brigs *Argus* and *Siren*. To replace Morris as commodore in the Mediterranean, Jefferson and Smith made what proved to be an inspired appointment: Edward Preble, famous for his command of *Essex* during the 'quasi-war' with France.

With *Constitution* as his flagship, Preble reached Gibraltar in September 1803. He had been preceded by the light frigate *Philadelphia* under Captain William Bainbridge, who was sent on ahead with *Vixen* to

Preble's abortive assault on Tripoli (4 August 1804) with USS *Constitution*, the only ship of force available to support the lightweight US squadron, at right. It was a forlorn hope: even the fire-power of *Constitution*'s broadside was not enough to silence the fire of the Tripolitan shore batteries.

waste no time in resuming the blockade of Tripoli. Preble meanwhile concentrated his force and entered Tangier, where he intimidated the Emperor of Morocco into agreeing a separate peace with the United States without American tribute or even the customary presents. Preble lingered to proclaim the blockade of Tripoli and set up a new cycle of convoys, then headed east – to receive the appalling news that *Philadelphia* was in Tripolitan hands. Bainbridge, chasing a blockade-runner too close inshore, had grounded her on the Kaliusa reef and had been taken into captivity with the whole of his crew, while the exultant Tripolitans refloated *Philadelphia*.

Preble's whole mission now hung in the balance, with the diplomatic triumph over Morocco abruptly wiped out by *Philadelphia's* loss. If *Philadelphia* could not be recovered by negotiation (and the Pasha dispelled that hope by demanding another American warship in exchange) she must be recaptured or destroyed. Preble took his time, maintaining the blockade of Tripoli throughout the winter of 1803-4 while he examined the problem for all angles. He negotiated the sending of supplies to the American prisoners in Tripoli, and corresponded secretly with Bainbridge (the latter using invisible ink). A shred of Credit was recovered by the capture of the Tripolitan ketch *Mastico* by *Enterprise*, the latter now commanded by Lieutenant Stephen Decatur, an officer of high ability. It was Decatur (another Marylander, born in 1779) who came up with the plan for destroying *Philadelphia* where she lay. There was no other option. With barely a thousand men under his command, Preble lacked the manpower to send in a cutting-out expedition of sufficient strength to recover *Philadelphia,* and another American repulse under the guns of Tripoli would be disastrous.

Decatur's plan was to use the captured *Mastico* (now renamed *Intrepid*) to approach *Philadelphia* without arousing undue suspicion; the Tripolitans would probably decide that the weak-kneed Americans had let her go. In support would be Stewart in the *Siren,* whose rig resembled that of a two-masted ship recently purchased by the Tripolitan agents in Sicily. A storming-party from *Intrepid* would then board *Philadelphia,* set her on fire, take to the boats and be brought out by *Siren*. Commanded in person by Decatur, the attack went in on the night of 16 February 1804 and was a complete success.

When the fire reached *Philadelphia's* magazine she blew up, and Decatur brought out the attacking party intact. He even saved *Intrepid,* which he had planned to use as a fireship if necessary. This feat earned Decatur immediate promotion to Captain as soon as the news reached home. But a hit-and-run operation of this nature was a far easier proposition than the close bombardment of Tripoli which Preble knew was essential, yet for which his ships lacked the necessary resources.

Preble's foremost need was for a friendly base of operations where American warships could repair and replenish without undue loss of time. With Britain and France at war again (the frail Peace of Amiens had expired in May 1803) the British at Malta had few spare facilities for the American squadron. This was a problem from which Morris, at least, had been mercifully spared. As a substitute, Preble turned to the vacillating Bourbon Kingdom of Naples with his eye on the ports of Sicily, its southernmost province. Before he could assault Tripoli, however, Preble needed the loan of gunboats and bomb vessels armed with mortars for precision bombardment, and when it came to these practical matters the professionalism of the Neapolitan Navy left much to be desired. In the end he secured the loan of eight Neapolitan gunboats, two of them bomb vessels, all manned by Neapolitan crews; but the summer of 1804 was well advanced before he judged his force to be ready to attack.

Preble finally launched his bombardment of Tripoli on 4 August 1804, pushing his gunboats inshore to close with the Tripolitan light craft and keeping *Constitution*, his only ship of force, ready to give fire support. Decatur, commanding a division of three gunboats, boarded and captured one Tripolitan vessel; in boarding a second he was momentarily overpowered, narrowly escaping death in a desperate hand-to-hand fight which became a favourite scene with American naval artists. Preble ventured inshore to sink two or three gunboats but *Constitution's* broadside, devastating though it was in frigate actions out at sea, lacked the power to destroy the all-important Tripolitan shore batteries. When an afternoon sea breeze set in, threatening to pen the attackers in dangerous shoal waters, Preble signalled the withdrawal of his force to the open sea.

Without the vital element of a landing force in sufficient strength to storm the forts, blow up the magazines and destroy the guns, there was little more that Preble's ships could do, and the Tripolitans knew it. With admirable pertinacity, however, Preble ordered his crews to repair battle damage and continue with successive day and night attacks throughout August, hoping against hope that the Pasha would lose heart and start negotiating. But it was not to be. The Tripolitans never dropped their guard enough to allow a really punishing attack to be made, and their gunnery certainly did not deteriorate. For what proved to be his last night attack (on 4 September 1804) Preble planned to send in *Intrepid,* packed with seven tons of powder charges, to explode amid the crowded shipping off the Tripoli waterfront, hopefully causing extensive damage in the city, and so cracking the Corsairs' morale. It may have been a moment's carelessness on the part of *Intrepid's* volunteer skeleton crew or it may have been a lucky shot from the shore, but *Intrepid,* which was certainly under long-range fire at the time, blew up before she was fairly into the harbor. Her brave crew – a dozen men commanded by Master-Commandant Richard Somers – had been sacrificed in vain.

It was the last disappointment for the gallant and capable Edward Preble. Though he had raised the discipline and morale of the Mediterranean Squadron to unheard-of-heights, he already knew that Commodore James Barron was on his way out to relieve him, under the inflexible promotion principle followed by the Department of the Navy in those early years. These constant changes of command were naturally the foe of continuity and tended to deny worthy officers the opportunity to overcome early setbacks. They did, however, have the advantage of exposing a wide range of officers on the Captains' List to the strains and stresses of high command and, though one unfortunate by-product was constant wrangling over seniority, the experience thus gained was a definite asset to the young US Navy. Unfavorable weather prevented Preble from launching a last attack on Tripoli before Barron arrived with no less than four frigates – reinforcements which Preble would have found invaluable the month before. In mid-September 1804 Preble, already suffering from the illness which was to result in his untimely death in 1807, sailed for home.

Barron, whose most powerful ships in late 1804 were *President* and *Essex,* had entered the US Navy in 1798 at the age of 30. High-quality service under John Barry in *United States* had won him early promotion, but his performance in the Mediterranean belied his first impression in naval service. Barron had little of the natural leadership qualities of Preble, let alone the aggressive instinct and dogged endurance which Preble had displayed throughout his command. Ill health led Barron to conduct a distant blockade of Tripoli throughout the winter of 1804-5, and in the spring he handed over command to John Rodgers – the fifth American commodore appointed in as many years. It therefore fell to Rodgers to handle the naval end of the amazing combined operation which, after so many previous failures, brought the war with Tripoli to a successful conclusion in the summer of 1805.

The new plan was the brainchild of William Eaton, American consul in the Mediterranean since 1799. Eaton proposed a flanking march against Tripoli from Egypt, using an Arab army raised in the name of Hamet Pasha, brother and rival of Tripoli's ruler, Yusuf Pasha. Eaton eventually raised a motley force of about 400 Arabs, led by himself with a bodyguard of seven United States Marines. Supported at sea by *Argus, Hornet* and *Nautilus,* detached from the close blockade of Tripoli which Rodgers simultaneously resumed, Eaton's 'army' made an arduous 500-mile march along the coast to the Tripolitan outpost of Derna, and captured it on 27 April 1805. Two of the seven US Marines were killed leading the attack.

Unexpectedly assailed by land as well as by sea (he had no idea of the real weakness of Eaton's force) Yusuf Pasha immediately sued for peace. In an unprecedented gesture, Yusuf actually released the captives from *Philadelphia* before receiving the token ransom which the American negotiators agreed to pay. The less attractive side of the treaty with Yusuf, signed on 4 June 1805, was the prompt American abandonment of Hamet Pasha's cause and of Eaton's 'army' in Derna (though Eaton managed to get Hamet out by sea before Yusuf's warriors reoccupied Derna.) Apart from this disagreeable flash of *realpolitik,* the United States could claim to have won through to 'peace with honour' in their five-year struggle against the Corsairs of Tripoli.

The US Navy had learned much from the conflict, not only in practice but in theory. Bainbridge and his fellow captives had put their 19-month incarceration to excellent use, studying their trade with debates and lectures – the 'University of the Prison,' in

which a leading name was that of David Porter. And it is certain that without the considerable expansion of the American fleet during the war with Tripoli, the US Navy would have been in far worse condition to face its next major trial: the 'War of 1812' with Britain.

The War of 1812 was declared by the United States under the slogan 'Free Trade and Sailors' Rights.' Like the 'quasi-war' with France in the late 1790s, it resulted from American determination to pursue neutral trade and profit in a world at war, defying two superpowers each of which was trying to blockade the other into starvation at the cost of excluding neutral trade. Maritime grievances between the United States and Britain dated back even before the outbreak of the Revolutionary War in 1792-93. Though the US Navy also used flogging to enforce discipline, and continued to do so until 1861, the far harsher British naval discipline made American ships natural havens for British deserters, at a rate of about 2,500 per year. The British resented American refusal to give up such deserters on demand; the United States equally resented the peremptory British habit of stopping American ships to search for deserters and, as likely as not, forcibly impress 'volunteers' into the Royal Navy.

An early example of these tensions occurred in June 1807, when *Chesapeake* sailed from Norfolk, Virginia for the Mediterranean under James Barron. Even though this was a peacetime cruise, it soon proved that she was in no condition to cope with unexpected trouble. Off Cape Henry, *Chesapeake* was pounced on by the British frigate HMS *Leopard,* whose captain demanded the right to search for four British deserters. When Barron refused, *Leopard* opened fire, killing three and wounding 18; *Chesapeake,* her decks still cluttered with stores, was unable to defend herself. Barron surrendered, the British boarded her and hauled off four American crewmen identified as deserters. Though the *'Chesapeake* Incident' predictably aroused American public outrage, it was the end of Barron's active career, crowning his lacklustre performance in the Mediterranean. Suspended from duty for five years (though found not guilty of cowardice), Barron spent them with the French Navy, but was refused another command when he returned to the United States after the outbreak of war.

By no means all of the maritime outrages which led to the Anglo-American War of 1812 were British-inspired. This is the incident of 16 May 1811 in which the USS *President* chased and battered the British sloop HMS *Little Belt* in the belief that she was a marauding frigate.

Chesapeake's humiliation nevertheless gave timely warning of the likely penalty for unpreparedness by American warships and in the next Anglo-American naval incident of note, four years later, it was a very different story. In May 1811 Rodgers took *President* to sea to warn off the British frigate HMS *Guerrière,* which had been impressing American seamen off New York. Late on 16 May Rodgers sighted and chased a British warship which he believed to be *Guerrière* and came up with her after dark. An exchange of hails was followed by a totally one-sided gun action in favour of *President,* with each side subsequently accusing the other of having fired first. Daylight revealed that the British warship was not a frigate at all, but the puny 20-gun sloop HMS *Little Belt.* With a firepower advantage of nearly three to one, *President* was virtually unscathed but *Little Belt* was badly cut up, with 11 dead and 21 wounded. Rodgers was exonerated by the subsequent Court of Enquiry, but the '*Little Belt* Incident' did nothing to modify Britain's high-handed attitude towards American shipping and neutrality.

These two incidents did not mean that British and American warships were invariably poised to fly at each others' throats; in the last five years of peace, there were occasional courteous exchanges between warships of the rival navies. In one such encounter, Captain Isaac Hull of *Constitution* and Captain James Dacres of *Guerrière,* over a glass of wine, discussed the fighting qualities of each other's ship and good-humoredly wagered a hat on which would win in a single-ship action. That friendly bet on a theoretical encounter was destined to become grim reality only two months after the outbreak of war, reluctantly declared by President James Madison (who had succeeded Jefferson in 1809) on 18 June 1812.

Though American myth naturally prefers to cast the War of 1812 as the American David again gallantly defying the bullying British Goliath, as in the War of Independence, the reality was somewhat different. In 1775 the British Government had not been willing to negotiate reasonably on every American grievance, as it was in 1812. There was a good deal more greed in the American declaration of war in 1812 than Americans like to remember. The 1810 census had shown that the population of the United States, at 7,239,881, was about two and a half times greater than it had been in 1783;

conquering British Canada, with its population of half a million protected by no more than 4,000 British regular troops, seemed an easy prospect. It was all very well for the 'War Hawks' in Congress (a term with a disconcertingly modern ring) to claim that Britain was again locked in war with the whole of Europe, and that conditions were ripe for another British humiliation. But this was a false comparison: in the early 1780s American victory had been clinched by the French battle fleet. In June 1812, nearly seven years had passed since British naval superiority had been secured by Nelson's destruction of the French battle fleet at Trafalgar.

Of course there was an equal excess of confidence on the British side in 1812. After Trafalgar, a total victory over 33 Franco-Spanish ships of the line, it was impossible to envisage defeat by a navy consisting only of a handful of frigates, without a single ship of the line. After their roll of naval victories since the outbreak of the French Revolutionary War nearly 20 years before, few Britons remembered the occasions when isolated British warships had been beaten fair and square, in untimely encounters with superior American warships, back in the War of Independence. There was altogether too much over-confidence on both sides in June 1812, and both sides soon paid for it in full measure.

Madison's administration had even less idea of how to fight a naval war with Britain than the Continental Congress had had in 1775. At one stage he toyed with the idea of keeping all American warships in home waters to serve as floating batteries, but happily Captains Bainbridge and Stewart, who happened to be in the new capital of Washington at the time, talked him out of it. Madison's biggest problem was that the mercantile states of New England, cradle of the American Revolution, were firmly opposed to war and virtually opted out of it, trading with Canada and Britain throughout. As a result the main American squadron was at New York, under Rodgers: the frigates *President, United States, Essex* (completing repairs at the outbreak of war), and *Congress,* with the sloop *Hornet* and the brig *Argus.* The nearest British force was at Halifax, under Vice-Admiral Sawyer; it was known to consist of the ship-of-the-line *Africa* (64 guns) and about seven frigates, and Rodger's main concern was to get to sea and start raiding before the British force could come south and blockade him at New York. He sailed at once, leaving Porter in *Essex* to complete his repairs.

It was a sound move, but the first American brush with the British was not propitious. Only 36 hours after leaving New York, Rodgers sighted the British frigate *Belvidera* and gave chase in *President*. The excellently-handled *Belvidera*, though damaged, got clean away to Halifax with news of the American strength, while Rodgers was left to nurse a broken leg caused by the bursting of one of *President's* maindeck guns. He then set off on a 10-week Atlantic cruise, sweeping as far as Madeira, during which no more than seven small prizes were taken.

Meanwhile, the land war had opened disastrously. Without support from New England, the ambitious triple invasion of Canada planned with such confidence by the 'War Hawks' collapsed in ruin. The Great Lakes were commanded by British flotillas. The Indians beaten at the battle of Tippecanoe in November 1811 rallied, under their great leader Tecumseh, to the British. After the briefest foray into Canada, General William Hull retreated to Detroit. There he surrendered to a handful of British regulars on 16 August, appalled by the Indian threat to massacre the 5,000 American civilians in his charge. This disaster was echoed by setbacks at sea in the first two months of the war, with *Nautilus* sailing straight into British hands off New York; the brig *Viper* was captured off Havana after a seven-week cruise with no prizes, as was her sister-ship *Vixen*.

After such a dismal prelude the remarkable run of American naval victories which began in the third week of August 1812 appeared all the more dazzling, the news of the first breaking hard on the heels of the gloom caused by the fall of Detroit.

The first victory was that of Porter in *Essex* over the sloop HMS *Alert* on 13 August. By the time *Essex* was ready for sea after the departure of Rodgers, *Belvidera* had been chased off station and New York was momentarily unwatched. Porter therefore got away unmolested on 3 July and headed for Bermuda, planning to harrass British convoys in the Caribbean. He had the luck to fall in with seven troopships escorted by the light frigate HMS *Minerva*, eluded her in a well-judged night attack, and captured a troopship with 200 soldiers. He took eight further prizes before falling in with *Alert* on the 13th and smashing her with two broadsides; the British captain surrendered to

avoid a useless slaughter. The captured *Alert*, once repaired, was used as a cartel to convey prisoners to Halifax under parole while *Essex* headed for home, taking a tenth prize before returning to New York on 7 September.

The news of the capture of *Alert* by Porter broke a week after Isaac Hull – nephew of the man who had surrendered Detroit – had brought *Constitution* into Boston with stunning news of his own: a crushing victory over the British frigate *Guerrière* on 19 August. Hull had sailed from Annapolis on the Chesapeake three weeks after the declaration of war and had headed north, hoping to join Rodgers whom he knew to be at sea. But what he actually sighted on 17 July was the British squadron from Halifax, commanded by Captain Philip Broke: the 64-gun *Africa* and frigates *Guerrière*, *Belvidera*, *Shannon* and *Aeolus*. A prolonged spell of still weather left *Constitution* becalmed just outside gunshot and an agonising three-day chase en-

Captain William Bainbridge, whose timely eloquence dissuaded President Madison from keeping the warships of the US fleet in home waters to serve as floating batteries.

sued under tow, with boats' crews trying to close within range on the British side and escape on the American. Hull, using the superior technique of kedging (winching his ship up to alternating anchors instead of relying solely on the muscle-power of his boats' crews) edged *Constitution* gradually out of reach and, as soon as the wind returned, sailed clean out of sight of his pursuers. It was a convincing demonstration of American seamanship and the impressive sailing qualities of the US Navy's big frigates.

After escaping from Broke, Hull put in at Boston to replenish the 10 tons of water pumped overside during the chase. He then headed for Nova Scotia and the Gulf of St Lawrence, beat up British shipping for just long enough to draw Broke's squadron north from American waters, then set off south to shift his hunting-ground to Bermuda – the natural tactical thinking of a born commerce raider. But on 19 August, a month after they had last been seen vanishing astern of *Constitution,* a familiar set of topsails was sighted. They were those of *Guerrière,* detached by Broke to return to Halifax. Now that prewar bet between Hull and Dacres was put to the test, with much more at stake than a hat.

Dacres' only real hope was that superior British gun drill, yielding a higher rate of fire, would cancel *Constitution's* much heavier broadside (about 684 lbs to *Guerrière's* 556). In going for speed, however, the British frigate's accuracy suffered badly, her all-important first broadside missing completely. As it happened, the decisive factors were superior American ship-handling and strength of construction; it was in this fight that *Constitution* earned the deathless nickname of 'Old Ironsides' from her apparent immunity to British shot. After a 15-minute cannonade, broadside to broadside, *Constitution* had only suffered minor damage aloft and light casualties; *Guerrière's* casualty rate was far higher, due to splinter wounds from her smashed scantlings. Her mizzenmast was the first to go, slowing *Guerrière* and allowing Hull to swing *Constitution* across his enemy's bows, raking *Guerrière* from stem to stern with two devastating broadsides. For a moment the ships hung clipped together, with *Guerrière's* bowsprit caught in *Constitution's* mizzen rigging. The last British guns able to fire and bear started a fire in Hull's cabin, but this was quickly extinguished. Then the ships tore free, leaving *Guerrière* a dismasted, beaten wreck.

Having done all that duty demanded, Dacres wisely surrendered. The two captains met again, and Dacres offered his sword to the victor. Hull declined, telling Dacres to keep it after such a gallant fight – 'but I will trouble you for that hat.'

Guerrière was so badly damaged that Hull had no choice but to take off the British wounded and survivors (*Guerrière* had lost 78 killed and wounded out of 272) and set her ablaze. Instead of continuing his cruise and hoping to offload his captive passengers on to prizes, Hull humanely headed for Boston where he arrived, to wild acclaim, on 30 August. Viewed coldly, ship for ship and gun for gun, the *Constitution/Guerrière* fight was not that remarkable an achievement – certainly not when compared with the circumstances of the *Bon Homme Richard/Serapis* fight back in 1779. What made the capture of the *Guerrière* an historic event was its timeliness, instantly dispelling the gloom caused by the preceding run of American failures. Arguably the most surprising aftermath of the encounter was the fact that Hull was never given another fighting command, though he lived until 1843 – yet another instance of the Department of the Navy's misuse of its best commanders.

The next encounter was unique, the only occasion when an American warship has captured an enemy warship, only to be captured itself within hours. Fleeting though it proved, the new victory was won by Master Commandant Jacob Jones in the sloop *Wasp,* working the Gulf Stream trade route between Halifax and the West Indies. On 18 October Jones sighted a British convoy escorted by the brig HMS *Frolic,* commanded by Captain Whinyates. Both warships had suffered rigging damage in a storm on the previous day but *Frolic* had come off worst, having her mainyard brought down. This naturally proved a considerable handicap in the ensuing action, competently won by Jones with his superior fire-power. *Wasp* was still standing by *Frolic,* with the American prize crew making repairs in the captured brig, when the British ship-of-the-line *Poictiers* (a '74') hove into view, heading for Bermuda. Because of their storm and battle damage, plus boisterous weather conditions which perfectly suited a ship-of-the-line, *Frolic* was soon recaptured and *Wasp* taken. Jones and his men, however, were returned to New York under cartel and were received as heroes, their surrender forgotten in the light of their earlier victory. At least they

had managed to tie down a vital British '74' to the tedious and distracting job of rounding up *Frolic's* convoy and seeing it safely to Bermuda.

Meanwhile two other sorties had been made by Rodgers with *Congress* and *President,* and Decatur with *United States,* with *Argus* in company. This imposing force sailed from Boston on 8 October, dispersing three days later once it was safely out to sea. Rodgers again had bad luck in not falling-in with any major convoys on a huge Atlantic sweep – south of the Azores to the Cape Verdes, and back by way of Bermuda – which lasted to the end of the year. In all this time he took only two prizes, though one of them turned out to be a bullion ship with nearly $200,000 on board. It was Decatur who had the real luck. After parting company with Rodgers on 11 October he headed towards Madeira in *United States* while *Argus* turned south to work the South American coast. Approaching Madeira on 25 October he

sighted the British frigate *Macedonian* (38), heading west to join the British West Indies Command. To Decatur's relish, *Macedonian's* Captain Carden wasted no time to coming in to attack.

Carden was foolish in doing this, for *United States* held all the hitting-power. Her broader beam made her a much steadier gun platform and her heavier guns had a longer range. *Macedonian's* only real advantages were greater speed and the upwind position or 'weather gauge,' possession of which enabled the owner to dictate the opening stage of the battle. Both these advantages were thrown away by Carden's gallant but stupid attempt to close the range at once, enabling *United States* to maul *Macedonian* to a wreck. *Macedonian* lost 100 men killed and wounded (over one-third of her crew); her mizzenmast, maintopmast and foretopmast were shot away, and 12 of her guns were knocked out. *United States* suffered only 12 casualties overall and her most serious damage was the loss of her mizzen topgallant mast. Decatur did not have to prolong the slaughter. He indicated that he was able and ready to take up a raking position and Carden, now completely unable to defend himself, surrendered.

Unlike *Guerrière*, *Macedonian* had been refitted shortly before the action. Though holed below the waterline, she still had two lower masts standing and was not in a sinking condition. Decatur therefore transferred a prize crew which succeeded in bringing *Macedonian* into Newport under jury rig, himself returning to New England with *United States*. Repaired and refitted at New York, *Macedonian* became the first command of Jacob Jones, former commander of *Wasp*, who was promoted Captain on his return from British captivity – another notable contrast with the churlish treatment accorded to Isaac Hull.

Decatur's capture of *Macedonian* coincided with the second war cruise of *Constitution*. She was now commanded by Bainbridge, who sailed from Boston on 26 October with the sloop *Hornet*. The latter was commanded by Master Commandant James Lawrence, noted for having been Decatur's second-in-com-

Another view of the duel between USS *United States* and HMS *Macedonian* in October 1812. Apart from her short-torn sails the US frigate appears unscathed as the rigging of her British opponent dissolves in ruin. .

mand during the burning of *Philadelphia* at Tripoli. Bainbridge had hoped to sail in collaboration with Porter and *Essex,* but the latter was not ready for sea until a fortnight later. Bainbridge therefore forwarded rendezvous instructions to Porter and sailed without him, planning to work the South American trade route. At Bahia, Bainbridge left Lawrence to blockade the British sloop *Bonne Citoyenne* (which was laden with bullion and therefore sensibly declined Bainbridge's challenge to come out and fight *Hornet*). On 29 December he was cruising offshore, on the lookout for possible prizes, when he sighted the British frigate HMS *Java,* under the command of Captain Lambert.

Lambert was not on the hunt for American raiders as he was on his way out to the East Indies, carrying a reinforcement draft of seamen, naval building materials, the new Governor-General of Bombay and several civilian passengers. He was calling at Bahia to top up with water before picking up the south-west trades for the long haul down to St Helena and the Cape of Good Hope. Like *Guerrière, Java* was French-built (the former *Renommée,* captured off Madagascar in May 1811). Like *Macedonian,* she was newly refitted and faster than her more powerful American opponent. Bainbridge countered this by setting his maincourse and forecourse (the big 'driving' sails, usually kept clewed-up during action). The gamble paid off. With her edge in maneuverability blunted, *Java* was unable to get across *Constitution's* bows or stern for a raking attack; instead she was subjected to another merciless American cannonade.

This was the toughest fight yet, with *Java* shooting away *Constitution's* wheel and forcing Bainbridge to con his ship with a chain of men passing orders to crews on the relieving tackle at the tiller. Then *Java's* headsails were left dangling when her jib-boom and bowsprit were shattered – a crippling loss of maneuverability. Lambert's only chance now was to close and board, but *Java's* faltering lunge at *Constitution* missed, enabling *Constitution* to rake her twice, bow and stern. Lambert fell mortally wounded and *Java's* First Lieutenant, Chads, accepted the inevitable and surrendered. An important American bonus was the capture of *Java's* codebooks and despatches which Chads, who was also wounded, had no time to drop overside. Bainbridge himself had been wounded twice. He decided that the battered *Java* was not worth saving, and burned her on 31 December. After landing his prisoners at San Salvador (where Captain Lambert died of his wounds) Bainbridge left Lawrence to continue the cruise and returned to Boston, arriving on 27 February 1813.

Three weeks later, Lawrence brought *Hornet* into Martha's Vineyard with $20,000 in captured bullion and news of yet another victory, which he had won on 24 February. Lawrence had kept *Hornet* at the mousehole outside Bahia, watching *Bonne Citoyenne,* until the arrival of the British '74' *Montagu* forced him to escape north-east along the Brazilian coast. As he prepared to round the 'corner' of Brazil at Pernambuco, Lawrence encountered and took the bullion brig *Resolution,* then headed for the Guianas. His plan was to seek what he might devour along the Guianan coast, then try out the West Indies on the voyage home. Off the mouth of the Demerara River in British Guiana, *Hornet* had additional luck by falling in with the British brig *Peacock.*

This was an interesting battle in that both ships were armed with carronades: short-range battering guns, known as 'smashers' in the Royal Navy, useless for long-distance sparring and disabling fire. Despite the fact that *Peacock* was a far flimsier vessel than *Hornet,* the British Lieutenant William Peake displayed all the bull-at-a-gate rashness which had undone Carden of *Macedonian* in the fight with *United States.* Peake's rapid approach was suicidal. Much better handled than the British ship, *Hornet* swung in close off *Peacock's* quarter (where hardly a British gun could bear) and hammered her defenseless and sinking in less than 15

One of the most devastating encounters of the War of 1812: the attack by USS *Hornet* on the British brig HMS *Peacock* which left the British ship defenceless and sinking in less than 15 minutes.

minutes. *Peacock* sank so rapidly that she took with her several members of the American prize crew sent across by Lawrence. *Hornet's* triumphant voyage home, with 277 men aboard (127 prisoners above *Hornet's* normal complement) was made in increasing hardship due to water shortage, victors and vanquished suffering alike.

Such was the fifth and last of an unbroken string of American single-ship victories over the Royal Navy, still justly remembered with pride by the US Navy. In these repeated humiliations of the most powerful navy on the planet, it may be said that the US Navy had truly come of age. And yet, lumped together and weighed against the overall war situation, the American naval successes came to very little. They were really only a fivefold fleabite against the massive strength of the Royal Navy – now fully on its guard and hot for revenge – which by February 1813 had hardly begun to deploy its full strength against the United States. The British reinforcements already sent across the Atlantic were formidable enough. Deployed from Halifax to Brazil, it all came to 17 '74s', two 50-gun ships, 27 frigates and 56 sloops, brigs and smaller warships – odds which the US Navy, for all its mood of justified triumph, could never hope to beat.

A British blockade of increasing severity was already withering American coastal trade and communications. The Federal Government was facing bankruptcy, and it was becoming harder and harder to repair and replenish the US Navy's warships between cruises. There was no hope of any early end to the conflict, and no hope of any delivering battle fleet and expeditionary force coming from France, as in 1779-81. The only real comfort was that with Napoleon still unbeaten in Germany (despite the disastrous Russian adventure of June-December 1812) the main British Army was still pinned to Europe. Until this situation changed, the British would be unable to invade from Canada. If the United States could win command of the Lakes, the British would not be able to invade at all.

In 1813 the balance swung back in favour of the British. Rodgers sailed again with *President* and *Congress* on 23 April, but took only 12 mediocre prizes in five months. At New York, *Chesapeake* was painfully refitting after a four-month cruise in which only three prizes had been taken. Stewart in *Constellation* lay blockaded at Norfolk by a powerful British squadron; *United States* and *Macedonian,* under similar blockade in Long Island Sound, were soon abandoned and their

The unlucky ship of the US Navy's 'Original Six' frigates: USS *Chesapeake*, captured by HMS *Shannon* on 1 June 1813, under full sail.

crews transferred to other ships. Then, on 1 June 1813, came the famous fight outside New York between Captain Philip Broke of HMS *Shannon* and *Chesapeake,* now commanded by Lawrence. *Chesapeake's* men had only stayed with the ship in the hope of getting the pay due to them. Higher American morale might conceivably have checked the fury with which the British boarded *Chesapeake* and captured her, virtually intact, after less than 15 minutes' fight. Lawrence died with another of the US Navy's immortal slogans on his lips – 'Don't give up the ship'! Apart from Rodgers, only Commander William Allen in *Argus* managed to slip the British blockade, in June 1813; after a promising cruise in the Irish Sea, destroying 19 ships in 31 days he was captured off St David's Head in August 1813 by the British brig HMS *Pelican.*

The only notable American naval victory in 1813 was the battle of Lake Erie on 10 September, which took place nearly 500 miles from the open sea and was won by Commodore Oliver Hazard Perry. Both the British and American flotillas consisted of two square-rigged brigs and a motley collec-

tion of schooners and gunboats, all built on the Lake from local green timber. Perry's flagship *Lawrence* was disabled at the start of the battle but he shifted his flag to *Niagara,* resumed the attack, and won through by superior weight of shot. Twelve months later, on 11 September 1814, a second American victory on Lake Champlain, won by Commodore Thomas Macdonough in his flagship *Saratoga,* rendered the Canadian frontier virtually secure. The solid gain of the Lake Champlain victory amply compensated for the British 'hate raid' of 24 August 1814, in which Washington had been burned. Three days after Lake Champlain, the gallant defence of Fort McHenry not only foiled the British attempt to give Baltimore the same treatment but also inspired Francis Scott Key to write *The Star-Spangled Banner,* in memory of how:

'... the rockets' red glare, the bombs bursting in air, gave proof through the night that our flag was still there.'

It was symbolic that the US Navy's proudest achievement in 1813-14 was the 17-month cruise of David Porter in *Essex,* although it did nothing whatsoever to relax the tightening economic stranglehold inflicted by the British blockade. After narrowly failing to make rendezvous with Bainbridge in December 1812, Porter decided single-handedly to extend the commerce war to the Pacific. This gave *Essex* a unique 'double': back in 1800 it had been the first American warship to enter the Indian Ocean by passing the Cape of Good Hope, and was now the first to enter the Pacific via Cape Horn. Displaying leadership, ingenuity and professional skills of the very highest, Porter kept *Essex* operational in the Pacific from February 1813 to March 1814, using a captured vessel renamed *Essex Junior* as a

tender; but in all those months he only managed to take 15 prizes. Crippled by weather damage, *Essex* was finally brought to action by the British frigate HMS *Phoebe* off Valparaiso on 28 March 1814. It was the bloodiest single-ship action of the war, with Porter only surrendering after over half his crew had become casualties: 89 American dead, and another 66 wounded. Among the survivors was 13-year-old Midshipman David Glasgow Farragut, destined half a century later to become the foremost admiral of the American Civil War.

By the time *Essex* fought her last battle, Anglo-American peace negotiations had been under way for months. It was obvious that with Napoleon defeated at last (he finally abdicated on 11 April 1814) neither Britain nor the United States had anything to gain from a stand-off war which might drag on for years, with the rest of the world reaping the profits of peace. Though the Treaty of Ghent formally ended hostilities on 24 December 1814, it took time for the news to arrive in American waters. By the time it did, a final British amphibious assault had been repulsed by General Jackson at New Orleans on 8 January. Attempting to break out from Long Island Sound in *President,* Decatur had been captured on 16 January by HMS *Endymion, Pomone* and *Tenedos.* But the last word had gone to Stewart in *Constitution,* who on 20 February 1815 captured both the sloop HMS *Levant* and the corvette HMS *Cyane* off Madeira. To a large extent these final actions perfectly symbolised the futility of the Anglo-American conflict, fortunately destined to be the last of its kind.

One of the lesser-known axioms of naval history is that when peace breaks out, politicians usually overstep the mark when reducing their country's navy to a reasonable peacetime strength. It has been shown above (p.32) how this syndrome had, in the 1780s resulted in the early liquidation of the first Continental Navy. Between 1815 and 1818 the gigantic British fleet was reduced by two-thirds, and its manpower dropped from 145,000 to 19,000. It is easy to imagine the effects on the diminutive US Navy of peacetime economies on a similar scale; but in 1815 the US Navy was lucky. Encouraged by the disappearance of US warships from the Mediterranean during the War of 1812, the Barbary Corsairs had resumed their attacks on American shipping, this time with Algiers taking the lead.

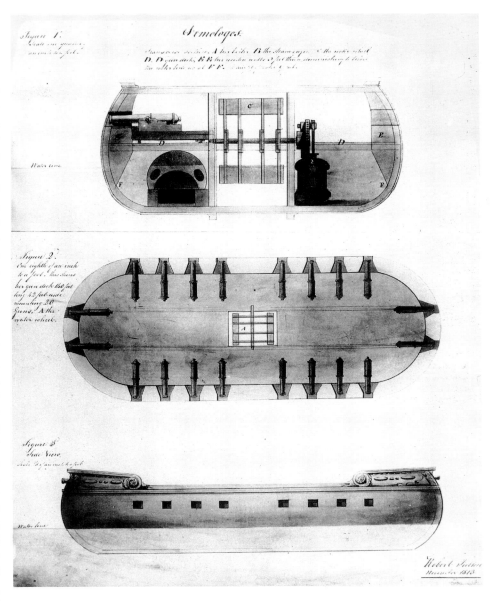

With memories of the Tripolitan War still barely ten years old, the Madison administration reacted with energy and promptitude. The right man was picked for the job, and given all the force and discretion he needed. Decatur sailed in May 1815 with a squadron ten strong (including the refitted British captures, *Guerrière* and *Macedonian*). This time there was no weak-kneed bargaining at the outset: Decatur settled the business

Above: Demologos (renamed *Fulton*), the US Navy's first steam 'warship', designed 1813. *Below:* End of an epic war cruise: USS *Essex* is captured by HMS *Phoebe* and *Cherub* off Valparaiso, 28 March 1814.

SQUADRON OF COMMODORE BAINBRIDGE

within ten weeks. On 17 June 1815, Captain Downes of *Epervier* (Porter's former First Lieutenant in *Essex*) captured the Algerine flagship *Mashuda,* the Algerine admiral being killed in the fight. Decatur then entered Algiers harbor and dictated peace terms, including a healthy cash payment of reparations to the United States; this was paid within the week. He then moved on to Tunis and Tripoli, in each case achieving the same result. By the end of June 1815 Decatur was free to return in triumph to the United States. By waging one of the briefest, most economical and effective naval campaigns in American history, he had safeguarded American Mediterranean commerce for the first decade of peace.

Decatur's success in the Mediterranean confirmed every essential point of President Madison's peacetime message to Congress, in which Madison affirmed that 'a certain degree of preparation for war is not only indispensable to avert disaster in the onset, but affords also the best security for the continuance of peace.' He was confident that Congress would in future continue to 'provide for the maintenance of an adequate regular force,' with particular regard to 'the gradual advance of the naval establishment.' Nor were these words spoken in vain. Twenty-one years after its foundation by George Washington, the US Navy had indeed come of age and the need for its continued maintenance was self-evident.

After 1815 there could be no doubting that the future of the United States, with immediate regard to the early break-up of the Spanish and Portuguese empires in Central and South America, would largely depend on the effectiveness of American sea power. The 'Monroe Doctrine' promulgated by Madison's successor in December 1823, warning off any European inclination to intervene in the development of the Americas, was less a statement of defiance than of confidence in this new role.

Above: The US squadron triumphantly cruises past Gibraltar in October 1815 after its resounding defeat of the Barbary Corsairs.

Left: 'A View of the Gallant Action between his Majestys ship the ENDYMION and the United States Ship the PRESIDENT' – 15 January 1815. Trying to break out from Long Island Sound, Decatur had damaged his ship in a temporary grounding on the eve of the action.

3: THE UNION PRESERVED 1823-1865

During the half-century which followed the peace of 1815, the US Navy enjoyed several advantages over its enormous British counterpart, and profited by them.

First and foremost, the US Navy was a young service. It was thus largely free of the more unfortunate encrustations of tradition which, throughout the 19th century, opposed change and sapped the fighting efficiency of the Royal Navy. To take just one example, the US Navy had gone into its first trial against France with nothing more inhibiting in the way of tradition than the example set by the sailors of the War of Independence. In 1797, on the other hand, the morale of the British fleet was shaken from top to bottom by widespread mutinies caused by miserable pay and ferocious discipline, very largely unchanged from the days of Cromwell in the 1650s. Not the least practical benefit of American independence was the US Navy's natural tendency, right from the beginning, to regard the Royal Navy as a useful model rather than an object for slavish imitation.

This tendency was, of course, most marked in the field of the technological improvements which completely transformed every class of warship by the end of the century. The US Navy was in the forefront of experiments with steam-powered vessels; then of steam-powered warships driven by screw rather than by paddlewheel; with guns firing explosive shell rather than solid shot; with ships protected by armor plate. The US Navy ended the century pioneering the fighting submarine, having joined with the British and French navies in rejecting submarines 80 years previously. From the 1860s the British repeatedly found themselves in the embarrassing position of building warships for foreign customers which were better vessels than those serving in, or even envisaged for, the Royal Navy. It was an embarrassment from which the US Navy was spared.

Certainly, during the years before transoceanic voyages under steam became truly practicable (about 1830-70), the US Navy had a vociferous cross-section of anti-steam diehards. The more vehement advocates — with no little justification in the early years — despised the newfangled steam 'teakettles' as detrimental to seamanship and pledged undying faith in 'ships of wood and men of iron.' But American naval conservatism never had the time to grow the deep roots of its British counterpart. It was not a century, and the United States was not a country — with its

phenomenal growth in territory, population and industry — which gladly suffered resistance to change. The American Civil War duly furnished the most devastating proof.

The US Navy enjoyed another important advantage over the British after 1815. Already swollen to massive proportions by the Napoleonic Wars, the Royal Navy's Admirals' and Captains' Lists set like concrete after 1815, due largely to the refusal of veteran officers to die off and make room for younger men. The results were naturally inimical to change and reform as well as being frustrating to new talent. The Royal Navy's performance in its next major test, the Crimean War of 1854-56, was predictably lackluster and, in at least one instance, positively unbalanced. (The British Rear-Admiral in the Far East, who had waited a soul-destroying *39 years* for promotion to the Admirals' List, went mad and shot himself on the eve of his first action in command.)

There was no such stagnation in the US Navy's pool of senior officers after 1815. The American service, until the Civil War, stuck to its original system of selecting 'Flag Officers' from the Captains' List to command the various active squadrons, and the Captains' List was nothing if not fluid. In 1820, for instance, Decatur was killed in a duel with Barron, who had never forgiven Decatur for giving what Barron regarded as malicious evidence during the enquiry into the *'Chesapeake/Leopard* Incident' back in 1807. The duel ended the careers not only of Decatur but of Barron (who otherwise might have hoped for a Flag Officer's command,) and of Bainbridge, censured for his insistence on acting as Decatur's second. Perry, the hero of Lake Erie, had died of Yellow Fever the year before, a victim of Venezuela's fight for independence from Spanish rule. (Perry had been on a mission up the Orinoco to persuade Simon Bolivar to refrain from attacking American ships with Venezuelan privateers.

Porter, of *Essex* fame, had the distinction of commanding the US Navy's first experimental steam 'warship,' the paddle-wheeler *Fulton,* in 1815. He then joined Hull and Rodgers as the first three members of the Board of Navy Commissioners. In 1823 Porter was appointed Flag Officer West Indies, but his excessive zeal in suppressing piracy in those waters (always a task rife with international sensitivities) earned him a court-martial and reprimand. He resigned from the US Navy in 1826 and served for the next three years as commander-in-chief of the Mexican Navy. The last 12 years of Porter's eventful life were spent as US Minister to Turkey; he died at Istanbul in 1843. Of the 'first-generation' heroes of the US Navy still alive in 1815, this left only John Rodgers, Thomas Macdonough (the victor of Lake Champlain) and Charles Stewart. Macdonough died in 1825 after a final seagoing command as Flag Officer Mediterranean and was succeeded in the Mediterranean by Rodgers, subsequently reappointed as a Navy Commissioner and serving until 1837, when he resigned on grounds of ill health; he died the following year. Charles Stewart, born in 1778 – who had first gone to sea as a merchant-service cabin boy before Washington's creation of the US Navy in the 1790s – alone lived on to become the US Navy's immensely respected 'grand old man,' outliving Isaac Hull, who died in 1843. A special Act of Congress created the post of Senior Flag Officer for Stewart in 1859; when the Civil War broke out in 1861 he lamented the fact that he was too old to go back to sea. It was fitting that he was appointed Rear-Admiral (retired) on the new List in 1862. He lived to see the victory of the Union he had served so well and died, full of honours, in 1869.

A healthy early clearance at the top of the Captains' List was matched by the service longevity of the frigates, the US Navy's staple warships. Though Congress had authorized the building of three ships-of-the-line during the War of 1812, these were never completed. Until the outbreak of the Civil War in 1861, frigates remained the heaviest warships in the American fleet — one of the most impressive characteristics of the US Navy, from its earliest years, being its knack of repeatedly renovating heavy warships for long-term service, giving the American taxpayer excellent value for money. (The most remarkable modern instance of this technique has been the appearance of the reactivated Second World War battleship *New Jersey* amid the 6th Fleet support force off Beirut in 1983-84.)

Two of the 'original six' frigates had been taken during the War of 1812: *Chesapeake* and *President*. Of the surviving four, *Congress* was broken up in 1834, the deterioration of her hull too far advanced to permit reconstruction. A second *Congress* was launched in 1841. A similar fate would have overtaken *Constitution,* condemned as unseaworthy in 1828, had there not been an immediate public outcry against the idea of

breaking up or selling 'Old Ironsides.' After reconstruction, *Constitution* returned to service in 1835 and remained with the fleet until 1860, when she was relegated to sail-training duties. *Constellation's* record was easily the best: she was still at sea, in the Mediterranean, when the Civil War broke out. Today lovingly preserved as national shrines, *Constitution* and *Constellation* are the only two frigates of the Napoleonic era left in the world.

United States was less fortunate. Unfit for sea in 1861, she fell into Confederate hands when Virginia seceded and was used as a Confederate 'receiving ship', or floating barracks, for the first year of the war. The Confederates burned her when they evacuated Norfolk in the spring of 1862. Her name has never been used since in the US Navy, though twice chosen for 20th century warships (a battle-cruiser and aircraft-carrier, neither of which was completed).

In any event, the survivors of the 'original six' frigates served the US Navy well for 40 years after the end of the War of 1812. It was not until 1854 that Congress authorized their replacement by six new frigates, named after rivers and powered by auxiliary steam engines. One of these, *Merrimack,* was destined to begin a new chapter in naval history by becoming the world's first fighting ironclad.

Though steam power was widely used in shallow-draught paddlewheelers for inshore work, the US Navy was still predominantly a sailing navy in 1861. So, for that matter, were the leading European fleets, in comparison with which the US Navy was by no means obsolete. It had made the vital transfer from solid shot to explosive shell, pioneered by the French General Paixhans in

The US Mediterranean squadron sails from Port Mahon in 1823. *Left to right: North Carolina* (flying the pennant of Commodore John Rodgers), frigates *Constitution* and *Brandywine*, and sloops *Erie* and *Ontario*.

the 1820s, and in this respect owed much to the calculations of J.A. Dahlgren, whose massive 'beer-bottle'-shaped guns were adopted in 1859. Once the Dahlgren gun was in service, it was only a matter of time before the US Navy followed the French and British in producing warships protected against explosive shell by armor plate. In the event, the US Navy Department ordered its first two ironclads, *Galena* and *New Ironsides,* in the summer of 1861 – only one year behind the British *Warrior* and two years behind the French *Gloire.* Yet, at the outset of the Civil War, the US Navy consisted of no more than

42 warships of all types.

This modest force had been more than enough for the US Navy's only 'shooting war' since 1815, the Mexican War of 1846-48. In this conflict the Navy's role was secondary to that of the Army: blockade and troop convoy followed by coastal support, one notable action being the forcing of the Tabasco River in 1847. (This was the war in which the US Marine Corps, serving with the Army, earned the second half of the battle honours remembered in the stirring Corps Hymn – 'From the halls of Montezuma to the shores of Tripoli'.) The main objective of the war was the conquest of New Mexico and California, and a squadron rounded Cape Horn to operate off the Californian coast. A leading light in this squadron was Commander Samuel Francis Dupont, born in 1803 at Bergen Point, New Jersey, who had joined the US Navy as a midshipman in 1815. In the Mexican War he distinguished himself as commander of the sloop *Cyane* in operations off San Diego and in the Gulf of California.

Apart from playing an active part in the crushing of piracy in the Caribbean in the 1820s, the US Navy's most enduring 'police duty' down to 1861 was the pursuit and

Above left: The steam frigate USS *Merrimack* as completed, before her half-burning and reconstruction as a mastless ironclad by the Confederates. *Below:* Union punch – an 11-inch Dahlgren gun on its slide-pivot mounting in an unidentified Northern warship during the Civil War.

interception of slavers. These operations were not limited to the African coast: they extended to the Caribbean and the Gulf, covering the slavers' home run to the markets of the Southern States. Anti-slavery patrols increased after the Northern crusade for the abolition of slavery got under way in the early 1830s – the powder-trail leading to the explosion of the Civil War. In directing anti-slavery patrols, the Federal Government had to walk on eggshells, wary of alienating either the Southern States or countries under whose flags slavers constantly sailed in camouflage. In 1847 the American Colonization Society finally achieved its aim of setting up a colony of freed African slaves on the west coast of Africa, the foundation of the Republic of Liberia. The commander of the American naval squadron entrusted with the job was Commodore Matthew Galbraith Perry, younger brother of the victor of Lake Erie.

Matthew G. Perry's greatest achievement, however, was his pair of missions to Japan (1852-53) in command of the East India Squadron, operating from Hong Kong. Perry's goal, the opening of diplomatic and commercial intercourse between the United States and Japan after centuries of self-imposed Japanese isolation, was brilliantly attained by the Treaty of Kanagawa on 31 March 1854. Much of Perry's success, which no career diplomat could have bettered, was due to the imposing appearance of his famous 'Black Ships': the steam frigates *Susquehanna* and *Mississippi,* aboard which the Japanese representatives were introduced to the delights of whisky and champagne. In his patient and sensitive negotiations, however, Perry took pains to give no impression of intimidation and succeeded by demanding nothing which the Japanese might regard as a national humiliation.

Apart from scoring one of the most important diplomatic breakthroughs of the century, the US Navy made a vital contribution to the dawning science of polar exploration. This was the first sighting and naming of the mainland of the Antarctic continent on 30 January 1840 by Commander Charles Wilkes (1798-1877). He was given command of an expedition of six sailing ships, headed by the sloop *Vincennes* and lamentably prepared for the rigours of Antarctic cruising, which sailed south in August 1838. In two Antarctic forays, separated by seven months of laborious repairs at Sydney, Wilkes followed 1,500 miles of the Antarctic coastline.

But Antarctic exploration was only one task in an immensely ambitious surveying cruise which extended to the South Pacific Islands and the length of the American western seaboard. It could hardly have been completed without the ferocious discipline upon which Wilkes insisted – and for which he was repaid, on his return to New York in June 1842, by court-martial charges of having exceeded his authority. Though acquitted, his troubles were not over: he was starved of funds with which to publish the full official account of the expedition. For all that – as Mark Twain bears witness in his autobiography, referring to his boyhood on the Mississippi – Wilkes became a national hero. Fame of a very different kind awaited him in the opening year of the Civil War.

Wilkes was not unique in his contribution to the enlargement of maritime knowledge and exploration. An equally famous name was that of Lieutenant Matthew Fontaine Maury (1806-73), who succeeded Wilkes as superintendent of the Navy Department's new Depot of Charts and Instruments. Maury's genius lay in charting and oceanography. In 1847 he produced his classic 'Wind and Current Chart of the North Atlantic', and in the following year produced its practical supplement: *Abstract Log for the Use of American Navigators.* Maury's sailing directions, based on the scientific exploitation of the predictable vagaries of wind and weather, yielded impressive savings in travel time and expense. Up-dated from observations sent him by the masters of ships, Maury's *Abstract Log* was republished in 1850 and 1851, and in 1853 Maury represented the United States at the great international conference on oceanography held in Brussels.

Maury's works earned him international fame and placed the United States in the front rank of maritime science. His system did for oceanography what the Swede Linnaeus had done for the classification of animals and plants in the previous century: it provided a comprehensive international framework for the advancement of science. Maury's crowning work, *The Physical Geography of the Sea,* appeared in 1855. Its practical yield was a profile chart of the Atlantic ocean floor between America and Europe, showing the feasibility of linking the continents with a submarine telegraph cable (achieved by the British in 1866). But for all his worldwide fame as a man of science, Maury considered himself first and foremost a Virginian. When, after months of hesitation, Virginia quit the Federal Union and joined the new 'Confederacy' of slave-owning states in April 1861, Maury resigned his commission in the Navy and went with her.

It was a decision taken with varying degrees of sadness and exultation by scores of other American naval officers, of both low and high rank. Some, indeed, jumped the gun, like Captain Franklin Buchanan of Maryland. Born in 1800 and joining the US Navy in 1815, he had risen to become flag captain and chief of staff to Perry during the 'Black Ships' mission to Japan, and had played a key role in the tricky negotiations with the Japanese. For this his reward was his appointment in 1854 as first Superintendent of the new US Naval Academy at Annapolis. When Abraham Lincoln was inaugurated in March 1861, as 16th President of a Union which no longer existed, Buchanan was in command at the Washington Navy Yard; his last duty there consisted of drawing up plans for the Yard's defense. Buchanan resigned his commission in the belief that his home state, Maryland, would follow Virginia into the Confederacy, and was not allowed to withdraw his resignation when she failed to do so. This error of judgement went almost unnoticed in the stream of miscalculations made by the Federal Government in 1861. Another seceding Marylander destined for high renown in Confederate naval service was 52-year-old Commander Raphael Semmes, who had distinguished himself at the bombardment of Vera Cruz in the Mexican War. Under the flag of the 'Stars and Bars,' Semmes was destined to become the most effective commerce raider before the German 'raider aces' of the two World Wars.

At its fullest, fleeting strength in the summer of 1861, the Southern Confederacy consisted of 11 states: South Carolina (the first to secede from the Union), Georgia, Florida, Alabama, Louisiana, Mississippi, Texas, Arkansas, Tennessee, North Carolina and Virginia. Apart from Maryland the three 'border states' of Kentucky, Missouri and Kansas, despite strong Southern sympathies, were kept in the Union; so were the mountain territories which formed the new State of West Virginia. The Confederacy was formed as the ultimate protest against what Southerners considered to be a tyrannical new Republican Administration, pledged to the abolition of slavery and the consequent destruction of the Southern way of life. The hopes of the South rested on the false belief that industrial Europe could not do without Southern cotton, and that the European powers would speedily recognise and support the Confederacy in its bid for independence.

Such foreign aid was vital, for in manpower and industrial resources the Confederacy never stood a chance against the North. The South's population was some 9 millions (of which 3.5 millions were negro slaves) against the 22 millions of the North. As for industrial establishments, the entire South could muster a grand total of no more than 16,896 against 99,564 in the North (with another 6,532 lost to the South in Kentucky and Missouri). In 1860, only one in ten of the total of manufactured articles turned out in the United States had been produced in the South. The same applied to the ships which carried the South's exports to the markets of Europe. Unless supplied from overseas the Confederacy would never be able, from its own resources, to replace the weapons and stores seized from Federal arsenals and shipyards after secession, once these had been expended.

On the other hand, the North could not mobilize all its undoubted resources overnight. The prewar US Army had barely topped 16,000 men in 1860 and 92 percent of them – 183 out of the 198 companies of regular troops – were garrisonned in the West and along the vast inland frontier. As for the naval front, the Confederacy's coastline stretched some 2,700 miles from the Rio Grande to the Potomac: a blockade-runner's paradise, against an enemy fleet no more than 40 strong at the outset of hostilities. The self-evident fact that the tiny US Navy could not support the Northern garrisons stranded, by secession, in Southern forts, led to the firing of the first shots of the war. This was the notorious bombardment of Fort Sumter at Charleston (12-13 April 1861).

Virginia's secession followed hard on the Northern surrender of Fort Sumter, and was the first real Northern defeat of the war. Virginia was not only historically the most prestigious of the Southern States, but the most advanced in population and industry. Richmond became the new Confederate capital. The Navy Yard at Norfolk, on the southern shore of the James River estuary, was hastily evacuated by the Federals but they held on to powerful Fort Monroe, north across Hampton Roads at the tip of the Yorktown peninsula. The big frigate *Merrimack* was still refitting at Norfolk and was

In the Civil War the North held nearly every card when it came to technological know-how. This imposing group shows Benjamin F. Isherwood (*seated at center*) with personnel of the US Navy's Bureau of Steam Engineering.

unable to escape to sea; the flustered Yard commander therefore ordered her to be burned and scuttled. This seemed infinitely preferable to allowing *Merrimack* to be captured intact, but it was, in fact, a fateful error of judgement. Though the flames destroyed her as a sailing ship above the waterline, *Merrimack* sank with her main hull and engines intact. Once the Confederates had raised her and pumped her out, they had the makings of a steam-driven ironclad warship – once they had found enough iron.

President Jefferson Davis's Confederate Government, taking up its duties in February 1861, was realistic enough to foresee the deadliness of a prolonged Union blockade, even if only applied at obvious pressure points like Hampton Roads. As Secretary of the virtually non-existent Confederate States Navy, Stephen Mallory of Florida was empowered to build and man ships able to challenge the Union blockade. He knew that any new warships built in the North were bound to follow the current European adop-

tion of ironclad warships, and insisted on 'the wisdom and expediency of fighting with iron against wood.' In this, Mallory was at least one jump ahead of his Northern counterpart, Gideon Welles, whose priority was commandeering enough suitable vessels to be armed as warships and sent out on blockade duties. By the time the US Navy asked shipbuilders to consider ideas for ironclads on the latest European model, it was August 1861 and the Confederate transformation of *Merrimack* was already under way.

With Norfolk separated from the Federal capital by less than 150 miles, it was not long before details of the new Southern ironclad began to filter north to Washington. Even when the wildest rumors were discounted, it was still clear that she was obviously being built for strength, and apparently more strength than that envisaged for the first Northern ironclads, *Galena* and *New Ironsides*. The Confederate Army had already shattered the first clumsy Northern invasion of Virginia, in the first Battle of Bull Run on

21 July 1861. In the shaken aftermath of Bull Run, the prospect of a Confederate ironclad able to break out from Norfolk and maybe even attack Washington was too awful to consider. The result was a panic search for an 'instant' Northern ironclad to set against *Merrimack;* and in October 1861 the US Navy decided that there was no choice but to gamble on the outlandish design for an ironclad 'monitor' (supervisor) put forward by the Swedish-born engineer John Ericsson.

Ericsson was, like Britain's Isambard Kingdom Brunel, one of the most versatile inventive geniuses of the new Industrial Age. By 1841, when he settled in the United States, he had designed railway locomotives and powered fire engines before turning his hand to screw-driven warships, naval shell-firing guns and their antidote: armor plate. In the 1840s he had built the first screw-driven warship for the US Navy (USS *Princeton*) only to fall out of favor when a gun designed (but not built) by him burst on her trials, killing two Cabinet ministers.

Still under a cloud in 1861, Ericsson was nevertheless consulted by Cornelius Bush-nell, the Connecticut shipbuilder who had won the contract for *Galena*. It was Bushnell who acted as go-between for Ericsson, urging the Navy Department to consider a cardboard model which looked like nothing on earth. It had no masts; it had no apparent freeboard; it had no conventional broadside of guns, but only two guns in a rotating pillbox turret. All the experts laughed Ericsson's model to scorn. But none of them could produce so much as a sketch for an ironclad which could be built in as little as 100 days (as Ericsson insisted was possible for his 'monitor'), and so wipe out the Confederate lead with *Merrimack*. It was to give the US Navy *something* with which to fight *Merrimack* that Ericsson was contracted, in October 1861, to build USS *Monitor*.

By this time the Confederate Navy had already given embarrassing proof of what it could do with conventional craft. CSS *Sumter* was the former mail packet *Havannah*, armed as a commerce raider with four 24-pounders and an 8-inch swivel gun. Under Commander Raphael Semmes, she slipped out of New Orleans in June 1861, easily dodging the lone USS *Brooklyn* patrolling

Forging the new steam-and-iron Navy – factory chimneys and gaunt new hulls at Washington Navy Yard, DC, about 1862.

the Mississippi approaches, and set off on a six-and-a-half-month commerce-raiding cruise through the Caribbean and Atlantic in which 17 Northern merchantmen were destroyed. By January 1862 the Confederacy had produced a commerce-raiding 'ace' fit to rank with the American naval heroes of the War of Independence and the War of 1812.

Moreover, by the fifth month of *Sumter's* cruise the Confederacy's wildest dream seemed on the verge of realization. The Northern blockade had laid heavy hands on a British ship, bringing the United States and Britain to the brink of war. The culprit was Captain Charles Wilkes, the former Antarctic hero. He had been at Norfolk when Virginia seceded, waiting to take command of *Merrimack;* instead he had had the job of burning her, before being appointed to *San Jacinto* and sent down to the Caribbean to hunt for Confederate blockade-runners. On 8 November 1861 Wilkes had stopped the British mail steamer and arrested two Confederate envoys (Senators James Mason and John Slidell) on their way to plead the Confederate cause in France and Britain.

It has been said that the absence of an Atlantic telegraph cable, providing a natural 'cooling-off period,' kept the peace; this was precisely the sort of act for which the two nations had gone to war in 1812. On both sides of the Atlantic the popular press yelped war-talk, hailing Wilkes as a hero in the United States and calling for direct action to avenge the insult in Britain. The two Governments showed far more sense, Whitehall accepting that Wilkes had not been carrying out deliberate orders and Washington releasing Mason and Slidell without a formal apology to Britain (the arrest having been disavowed). As for Wilkes, he was promoted Acting Rear-Admiral in 1862 and kept in the Caribbean to keep up the pressure on Confederate blockade-runners. (Undoubted success in this role did not, however, save him from court-martial two years later and conviction for 'disobedience, disrespect, insubordination, and conduct unbecoming an officer'. After one year's suspension from duty he was finally retired with the rank of rear-admiral in 1866.)

The New Year of 1862 therefore came in with Confederates beginning to accept that they were on their own, forced to save themselves by their own exertions without foreign aid; and the building race between *Merrimack* and *Monitor* continued apace. Inventing and correcting as he went along,

Ericsson proved as good as his word: *Monitor* was launched at New York on 30 January 1862. She was the first wartime naval achievement of the Industrial Revolution, her construction having been farmed out to different firms for the separate manufacture of hull, engines, turret, and armor plate – a facility denied the Confederacy, with its lack of industrial plant. Not surprisingly, *Monitor* was riddled with teething troubles (mostly concerned with the steering gear) and she was not ready to be towed down to Hampton Roads until 6 March. This enabled *Merrimack* (now re-christened CSS *Virginia*) to beat *Monitor* into action by less than a day.

The ungainly Southern ironclad had been rebuilt with a massive angled penthouse running fore and aft, of heavy timbers sheathed in armor plate (the latter mostly contrived from railway iron). She carried eight guns in broadside (four per side) plus a bow and stern gun, each of the latter swiveled for a choice of fire through three ports. Unlike *Monitor*, *Virginia* had been given an armored spur with which to ram enemy ships below the waterline: an attack technique wholly unsuited to sailing warships. *Virginia* was so unweatherly that she could only operate safely in a calm; a storm on 7 March (which all but sank *Monitor* on her way down from New York) delayed her first sortie by a day. But on 8 March 1862 *Virginia* became the world's first ironclad to go into action. Under Captain Franklin Buchanan, commanding the Confederate James River Flotilla, *Virginia* lumbered across Hampton Roads to sink the becalmed sailing sloop USS *Cumberland* with a ramming attack, then turned on the nearby frigate *Congress* and set her ablaze with shellfire and red-hot shot.

All this was accomplished in the teeth of point-blank fire from the Union ships and their covering shore batteries. *Virginia's* armor survived the lot, though Buchanan (venturing outside for a better view) was wounded by a rifle bullet; he was replaced in command by Lieutenant Jones. With evening approaching and the tide on the ebb, restricting *Virginia's* already limited maneuverability, Jones prudently decided to withdraw for the night and finish off *Minnesota, St Lawrence* and *Roanoke* on the morrow. As night fell, however, the insignificant shape of *Monitor* came steaming in past Fort Monroe, and daybreak on 9 March found her poised to defend *Virginia's* intended victims.

The extraordinary fight between *Virginia*

and *Monitor* on the forenoon of 9 March 1862, the first-ever battle between ironclad warships, ended with neither ship having inflicted vital damage on the other. *Monitor's* heavier guns were frustrated by *Virginia's* sloping armor. Though the two ships battered each other for three hours, there was only one serious casualty: Lieutenant John Worden, commander of *Monitor,* Momentarily blinded by a direct hit on the observation-slit through which he was peering. Until Lieutenant Greene took over command and brought *Monitor* back into the fight, *Virginia* seemed on the point of adding *Minnesota* to her tally of victims, but prudently retired again with the ebb of the tide, rather than risk being stranded. On balance *Virginia* had taken the heavier damage, with the muzzles of two guns shattered, her tall stack shot away and a leak in the bows from the loss of her ram during the earlier attack on *Cumberland,* aggravated by an abortive attempt to ram *Monitor.* Though *Monitor* had undoubtedly frustrated *Virginia's* attempt to break the Union blockade of the James River, the Battle of Hampton Roads ended in a stalemate which seemed destined to last as long as the two ironclads confronted each other.

The stalemate was abruptly broken in just over two months by the movement of the land armies, beginning on 4 April with a Northern advance on Richmond up the Yorktown peninsula. This forced the Confederates to evacuate first Yorktown and then Norfolk (4-10 May 1862). When it proved impossible

to move *Virginia* up the James to defend Richmond, she was set on fire and blown up by her crew on 11 May. Four days later her gunners helped repel an attempt by the US Navy to force open a direct route to Richmond up the James by bombarding and passing Fort Darling. The Northern flotilla consisted of *Monitor,* the new ironclad *Galena* and three gunboats, and its defeat revealed the limitations of ironclads when opposed by well-emplaced shore batteries. Hit 43 times, *Galena* was reduced to a wreck, her frail 4-inch armor shattered. She never saw service as an ironclad again. *Monitor* again came through unscathed, but her guns could not be elevated enough to silence the Confederate fire.

Richmond was saved by Robert E. Lee's victory in the Battle of the Seven Days (25

Above: Union gunboat USS *Choctaw* off the battered city of Vicksburg in 1863. *Below:* The distinctive pill-box turret of a Northern monitor: USS *Lehigh* in the James River, spring 1863.

Distinctive features of the river gunboats during the Civil War were the sloping, armoured sides of the casemate and broadside guns protected by armored ports. *Below:* The crew of USS *Cincinnati* take advantage of a quiet spell and good laundry-drying weather. *Right:* USS *Cairo* in more martial guise, 'showing her teeth' for the camera.

June-1 July 1862), after which the Union field army was withdrawn from the Yorktown Peninsula. Apart from a two-month withdrawal to New York for repairs, *Monitor* remained on the lower James River until December 1862. On the last day of the year, while attempting another sea voyage to join the naval blockade of Wilmington, North Carolina, *Monitor* foundered and sank off Cape Hatteras – a sad end to an astonishing operational career which . had changed warship design for good.

Whilst 1862 was a year of repeated Union frustration and defeat in the East, it was a very different story in the West. There the US Navy, though operating hundreds of miles from salt water, played a vital role in helping slice the Confederacy in two down the line of the Mississippi. The armored river gunboats of the North were essential in overwhelming or by-passing the Confederate strongpoints barring the southward Union advance.

Building the Union gunboat fleet was, like the breakneck construction of *Monitor*, another remarkable demonstration of the North's industrial muscle. It was achieved largely by the organising genius of millionaire industrialist James B. Eads, who masterminded the construction of seven new ironclad gunboats well within the promised 65 days. These were *St Louis, Carondelet, Cincinatti, Louisville, Mound City, Cairo* and *Pittsburgh,* built piecemeal in timber yards, foundries and workshops scattered across eight of the Northern states. Eads then added two more gunboats, one converted from a river salvage boat (*Benton*) and one

UNITED STATES MISSISSIPPI GUN-BOATS BEING BUILT AT CARONDELET, NEAR ST. LOUIS, MISSOURI.
[SKETCHED BY ALEXANDER SIMPLOT.]

Above: Mass production of Mississippi gunboats at the Eads works, Carondelet, Missouri, in October 1861. *Right*: The screw, unarmored under-hull and waterline armor belt of USS *Dictator*, probably photographed shortly before her launch on 26 December 1863 – Delameter Iron Works, New York.

from a ferry (*Essex*). All were broad in the beam, flat-bottomed stern-wheelers, known generically as 'Pook's Turtles' after Samuel M. Pook, the naval architect working in harness with Eads. Commanded by Flag Officer Andrew Foote, the Northern gunboat fleet mustered at Cairo, Illinois, to support the first drives against the Confederate river strongholds in the New Year of 1862.

The gunboats got off to a resounding start with the shattering bombardment which assisted General Ulysses S. Grant to capture Fort Henry on the Tennessee River on 6 February 1862. They moved to the Cumberland River to spearhead Grant's follow-up capture of Fort Donelson on 16 February, then returned to Cairo to make repairs before tackling the first major barrier on the Mississippi: 'Island Number 10', north-western bastion of the Tennessee frontier. Here, frustrated by the well-sited Confederate batteries, the Union advance stuck until *Carondelet* ran the gauntlet on the night of 4-5 April and silenced the guns preventing Union troops from crossing to surround the fortress. This early winning of Northern supremacy on the central Mississippi was followed at once by one of the US Navy's finest feats of the Civil War: nothing less than the capture of New Orleans, the Confederacy's second city.

The victor of New Orleans was 61-year-old Flag Officer David Glasgow Farragut, a veteran of the War of 1812 who had sailed the Pacific under Porter in *Essex,* and had been captured in her. The plan to take New Orleans was formed after the first Northern footholds on the Confederate Atlantic coast had been won with comparative ease: Hatteras Inlet (29 August 1861) and Port Royal (7 November 1861), followed by Roanoke Island on 7 February 1862. To tackle New Orleans, Farragut was given 10,000 troops and a fleet consisting of eight steam-powered warships,

nine gunboats and a flotilla of mortar schooners. None of these were ironclads, and when Farragut heard that the Confederates were building two large ironclads (*Louisiana* and *Mississippi*) for the defense of New Orleans, he decided to attack before they were ready. Farragut was not deterred by the pair of forts, Jackson and St Philip, commanding the channel leading north to New Orleans; he intended to pass them, not match them in fire-power, and he did just that. Within 24 hours after fighting his way past the forts, Farragut's ships anchored off the New Orleans waterfront to receive the surrender of the defenseless city on 25 April 1862.

By the end of June 1862 Fort Pillow and Memphis had followed New Orleans, Island No. 10 and Forts Henry and Donelson, and Confederate control of the Mississippi had shrunk to the three-mile waterfront of Vicks-

burg, Mississippi. Farragut had cruised up from New Orleans to join hands with the Northern gunboats, now commanded by Flag Officer Charles H. Davis – but, even when the two forces joined above Vicksburg, they proved unable to capture the town without a powerful land army attacking from the east. Silencing the guns of Vicksburg on their commanding bluffs above the town was a task beyond Farragut's warships and gunboats. As *Monitor* had discovered at Fort Darling on the James River, two months before, not even the most powerful ironclad could neutralize positions sited on high ground beyond the limited elevation of its guns. In October 1862 Farragut, now a rear-admiral, withdrew his seagoing ships to New Orleans. His replacement as the new Flag Officer on the Mississippi was the commander of his mortar boats during the

Victor of New Orleans and Mobile Bay: Admiral David G. Farragut strikes a suitably heroic pose beside the wheel of his flagship, USS *Hartford*, at Mobile in 1864. With Farragut is the bearded Captain Percival Drayton, USN.

Opposite, below: Northern and Southern gunboats clash at Memphis, 6 June 1862. At center, the USS *Monarch* rams the Confederate *General Beauregard*; the Confederate *General Price* can be seen at left, with the Confederate flagship *Little Rebel* in the background.

assault on New Orleans: David Dixon Porter, son of Farragut's old commander in the War of 1812.

The fate of the war hung in the balance from the high summer of 1862 to that of 1863. The string of famous Confederate land victories won in the East by Robert E. Lee and 'Stonewall' Jackson, went hand in hand with a succession of failures for the US Navy. On the high seas, Raphael Semmes was on the loose in a new Confederate raider, CSS *Alabama,* secretly built in Britain, which began a remarkable two-year cruise in August 1862 and destroyed 20 US ships in her

The Confederate ironclad Arkansas, at center, running through the Union fleet off Vicksburg, 15 July 1862.

THE GREAT NAVAL BATTLE BEFORE MEMPHIS, JUNE 6, 1862.—SKETCHED BY MR. A. SIMPLOT.—[SEE PAGE 410.]

first two months of operations alone. In January 1863 she sank the Union gunboat *Hatteras* off Galveston before extending her hunting grounds to the South Atlantic, Indian Ocean and China Sea – a range remarkable by the standards of the day, and destined not to be surpassed until the disguised German merchant-raiders of the two World Wars. In March 1863 Porter's gunboats, frankly attempting the impossible, failed to break through to the upper Yazoo River in Vicksburg's rear by forcing a channel from bayou to vegetation-clogged bayou. In the following month Rear-Admiral Samuel Du Pont, victor at Hatteras Inlet in November 1861, tried to take Charleston with a bold frontal assault by nine ironclads, seven of them turretted monitors. Though their armor stood up well to a formidable hammering by the guns of Fort Sumter and the other Charleston forts – they fired an astonishing 2,209 rounds to only 139 from Du Pont's ships – Du Pont was forced to order a humiliating withdrawal after two hours. Like Vicksburg, Charleston was a target beyond the US Navy's capacity and held out

until invested from the landward by the Army.

After the tide turned for good with the twin Confederate defeats at Vicksburg and Gettysburg in July 1863, the biggest threat to units of the US Navy was posed by weapons born of desperation: the mine and the torpedo (both referred to as 'torpedo'). Torpedoes of the Civil War were of the spar variety: extended from the bow of a fast boat, manned by what amounted to a suicide crew. The first Confederate torpedo attack was against *New Ironsides* off Charleston in October 1863, but though the ironclad's plates were started by the explosion the ship survived. It was a very different story with the wooden-hulled *Housatonic*, ripped open and sunk by a spar torpedo on 7 February 1864. A new factor had entered naval warfare. It was one which the Confederate Admiral Buchanan hoped would keep Farragut's fleet out of Mobile Bay, the last Confederate naval base on the Gulf by the summer of 1864.

Well aware of the 'torpedo' menace, Farragut was more concerned with running his

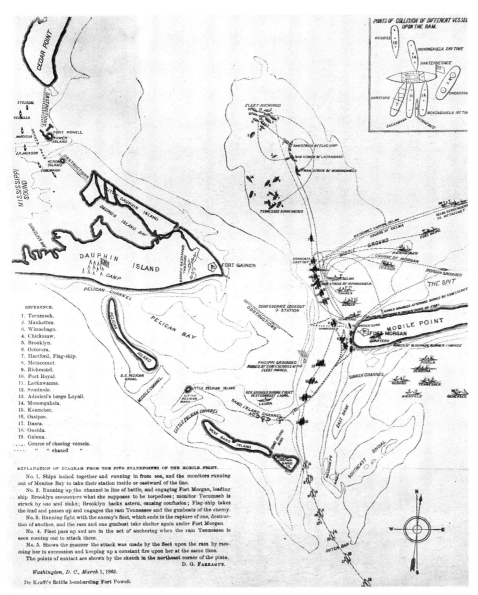

Map of the Battle of Mobile Bay (5 August 1864) showing Farragut's line of approach and *(inset)* the massive concentration of fire-power brought to bear on the Confederate ironclad *Tennessee.*

fleet in past Fort Morgan, guarding the entrance to the Bay. He used his four monitors as a line-ahead screen for his wooden ships, which he had lashed together in pairs for safety. This level-headed deployment had the desired result, with the monitors drawing the bulk of Fort Morgan's fire during the critical entry to Mobile Bay – but the Union fleet was thrown into momentary disarray when the leading monitor *Tecumseh* hit a 'torpedo' and sank with 93 of her crew of 114. Farragut rose splendidly to the crisis, giving the US Navy a watchword fit to rank beside 'Don't give up the ship!' and 'I have not yet begun to fight!' 'Damn the torpedoes!' he barked. 'Full speed ahead!'

Having failed to keep Farragut's fleet out of the Bay, Buchanan's last hope was the prowess of his flagship *Tennessee,* the South's last heavy ironclad – but she stood no chance against the terrible combined pounding, at point-blank range, by the Union monitors *Winnebago* and *Chickasaw.* After a heroic fight, with her steering gone and her armor

being blown off in great chunks, *Tennessee* surrendered and the battle was over.

The Battle of Mobile Bay on 5 August 1864 was the last fleet action of the American Civil War. It was fought two months after *Alabama* was finally caught off Cherbourg by Captain John A. Winslow of USS *Kearsarge,* and sunk after a no less dramatic single-ship action. Extraordinary honors

"BROOKLYN."   "ITASCA."   "RICHMOND."   "HARTFORD."   "CHICKASAW."

"TENNESSEE."   FORT MORGAN.

NDER OF THE "TENNESSEE," BATTLE OF MOBILE BAY.

were paid to Winslow by a grateful government, as had been paid to Britain's Captain Broke after his capture of USS *Chesapeake* in 1813. Apart from an immediate promotion to Flag Officer and unusually early postwar advancement to Rear-Admiral, Winslow was ordered to be kept on the active list for the rest of his life.

When Lee's Army surrendered to Grant at Appomattox on 9 April 1865, the US Navy could claim to have played a full and varied part in the victory of the Union. Indeed, no other Navy had ever been forced to undergo a greater transformation in a mere four years of war. It now remained to be seen how much of this impetus would be lost, and how much retained, as the battle-scarred American nation prepared to heal its wounds in peace.

Position of the ships at the moment of *Tennessee*'s surrender, hemmed in on all sides.

81

4: IRONCLADS AND DREADNOUGHTS 1865-1918

In the summer of 1865 the US Navy was taking stock after one of the most remarkable transformations ever experienced by any navy in so short a time. Only four years before, on the brink of the Civil War, the US Navy had been no more than a numerically modest fleet of sailing wooden warships with auxiliary steam power. After the war, thanks to the first total harnessing of the Industrial Revolution to meet the demands of modern sea power, the US Navy found itself leading the world in the development of armored steam warships with turretted gun armament – and these new warships were only part of the story. The American Civil War had proved that mine warfare, first used with any effect in the Crimean War of 1854-56, was much more than a worrying novelty: it now had to be considered an integral part of naval warfare. So had the torpedo-boat, though admittedly to a lesser degree (until the British perfected the self-propelled torpedo in the 1870s). After its loss of the wooden *Housatonic* to a Confederate torpedo-boat in February 1864, the US Navy had used a torpedo-boat to sink the Confederate river ironclad *Albemarle* on the Roanoke in October of the same year, proving that ironclads were no more proof against torpedo attack than wooden warships.

Though nearly all these lessons had been learned in coastal and riverine waters, the Civil War had also proved that steam power, armor plate and heavy-caliber gunnery were perfectly suited to the ancient ploy of commerce-raiding. In a way, the depredations inflicted by the Confederate commerce-raiders *Sumter, Alabama, Florida* and *Shenandoah* (the last-named of which was still at sea when the war ended) were a more valuable experience to the US Navy than

that gained with the new ironclad types. They were a reminder that the US Navy must retain an oceanic cruiser force for the defense of the sealanes against enemy raiders – and that these cruisers (like mine warfare, the name 'Cruiser' in its modern sense dated from the Crimean War) had to be of the most modern and best-armed type. *Alabama* and *Keasarge* had fought their famous duel off Cherbourg under steam; *Alabama's* fate had been sealed by a heavy shell bursting in the engine room, whereas the Union captain had cannily contrived a measure of armored protection by draping his anchor-chains over the side.

As a final example of what the US Navy had learned from the Civil War, mention should be made of the *Dunderberg*, the enormous Union ironclad nearing completion at New York when the war ended. *Dunderberg* ('thunder mountain') was 373 feet (114 meters) long – 50 feet (15.2 meters) more than Brunel's famous iron liner *Great Britain* – and was designed to carry two revolving gun casemates as well as broadside batteries under an angled penthouse. From her bow there jutted an awe-inspiring ram shaped like a plowshare. With her low silhouette, sloped armor and ferocious ram, *Dunderberg* would probably have proved a match for the heaviest battleship anywhere in the world.

However, for the postwar US Navy, inevitably shrunk by a cost-conscious administration struggling with a wealth of domestic crises, there was no place for a monster like *Dunderberg*. She was eventually sold to the French Navy, whose warship design over the ensuing 30 years bore the unmistakable stamp of *Dunderberg's* influence.

Despite all these undoubted improvements brought about by the Civil War, the postwar US Navy nevertheless fell victim to an unfailing natural law. Any fighting service raised to an unprecedented state of development by the pressures of war inevitably suffers from the ensuing peace, with its automatic tendency towards demobilisation, retrenchment, domestic reconstruction and economy. In the case of a navy, these peacetime influences wither the size of the fleet, its trained manpower and consequently its combat experience (the most rapidly waning asset of them all). No less is true of the will to improvise and innovate, which had applied to the naval war of 1861-65 far more than to land warfare. An automatic extension of this natural law is that the longer the peace endures, the more damaging its effects will

Previous pages: The shape of things to come – one of the Confederate submersibles or 'Davids' driven by steam or an eight-man hand-cranked shaft, with the spar for its torpedo at right, beached at Charleston at the end of the American Civil War.
Below: First warship lost to submarine attack was the unarmored USS *Housatonic*, sunk by a hand-driven 'David' on 7 February 1864.

be on the fighting services.

The US Navy was saved from the worst results of this syndrome by the increasing awareness of its strength and potential as a world power with imperial interests. The purchase of Alaska and the Aleutian Islands from Russia in 1867 could be said to have an obvious precedent in American history: the purchase of the Louisiana territory from Napoleon's France in 1803. But the Louisiana Purchase had only facilitated the exploration and settlement of the continent west of the Mississippi. The Alaska Purchase gave the United States a vital stake in the North Pacific, and this was reflected in the same year, 1867, by the securing of American rights over the Midway Islands, 1,200 miles west of the kingdom of Hawaii. Eight years later, in January 1875, the United States negotiated a 'reciprocity treaty' with Hawaii, admitting Hawaiian sugar into the United States free of duty – but in exchange rapidly reducing the islands to economic dependence on the United States. In 1887 the treaty was

extended, giving the US Navy the use of Pearl Harbor, where the building of a naval station with coaling facilities rapidly followed. The next step, in January 1893, was the landing of US Marines to defend American residents in Hawaii against the results of growing constitutional unrest; this was followed by the American establishment of a Hawaiian Republic (July 1894) and the final ratification of a treaty of annexation with the United States by the Hawaiian Senate in June 1897. The Hawaiian Islands were formally transferred to the United States in the following August – a classic pattern of imperial expansion which Americans, naturally prone to sneers at *British* imperialism, would do well to remember.

This new role for the United States as a North Pacific power, no more than a debating-point before the Civil War, effectively cancelled domestic pressure for really damaging service economies. It led to the rapid development of San Francisco as the permanent 'rear base' of the US Pacific

Replete with battle honors: Farragut's flagship USS *Hartford*, completed in 1859, showing her starboard battery of 9-inch Dahlgren guns.

Below: Paving the way to an American 'Two-Ocean' battle fleet – the coastal battleship USS *Iowa* (BB.4) as completed, before a towering 'cage' mainmast was installed aft of the stacks. Launched in 1896, *Iowa* served through the First World War in the training role, being expended as a gunnery target in 1923.

Squadron, with other naval bases subsequently added at Bremerton, Puget Sound, to the north and finally at San Diego to the south. By the middle 1890s, the transformation of the US Navy into a permanently 'two-ocean' navy was an accomplished fact.

Though the enduring years of peace saw the lead in warship and gunnery design recross the Atlantic to Europe, this also had direct advantages for the US Navy. With money kept tight by Congress, American designers were denied the costly interim experiments made by their European counterparts. British and French designers came up with many a weird and wonderful hybrid design between 1865 and 1885, as the full sailing-ship rig of masts and yards passed into final obsolescence. The US Navy Department could afford to lie back and opt for the best of the European designs for application to American needs – and this by no means implied excessive reliance on European experience.

One of the greatest American naval assets in these years was the remarkable shipbuilder Charles H. Cramp (1828-1912), who gave the US Navy an invaluable continuity in ship design from the ironclads of the Civil War to the battleships and cruisers of the

Dreadnought era. Cramp had given the US Navy its first seagoing ironclad, *New Ironsides,* in 1862; 30 years later, with *Indiana, Massachusetts,* and *Iowa* (BBs. 1-3, laid down 1891-93) he produced the first modern American battleships. These were only the precursors of four more battleships built at Cramp's Philadelphia yard before his death: *Alabama* (BB.8), *Maine* (BB.10), *South Carolina* (BB.26), and *Wyoming* (BB.32) – the latter a full-blown Dreadnought with twelve 12-inch guns.

No less important, though overshadowed in the prevailing anxiety not to be outstripped in the development of conventional sur-

Above: A typical cruiser of the post-Civil War years – USS *Richmond* as she looked after receiving an 8-inch rifled pivot gun in her refit of 1877-78, and before her bridge was rebuilt forward of the stack in her refit of 1884-87.

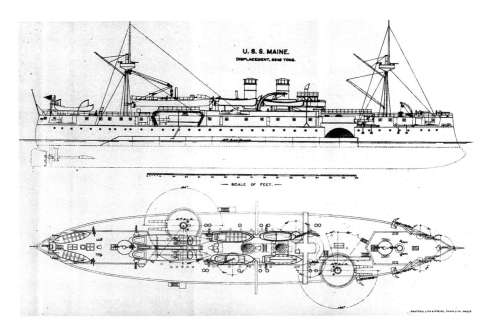

U. S. S. MAINE.
DISPLACEMENT, 6640 TONS.

— SCALE OF FEET —

Above: Melting-pot years in battleship design, midway between broadside and center-line turret armament. This plan for the ill-fated USS *Maine* (1839) placed the turrets in wing mountings instead of on the centerline.

Below: Blueprint for the future. Only five years later, the lines of the *Holland VIII* already anticipated the streamlined 'teardrop' hull familiar in US submarines of the 1980s.

face warships, was the American inventor John P. Holland. He provided another direct link with the lessons of the Civil War by building on the experience gained by the Confederate 'Davids': the semi-submersible torpedo-boats which had attacked *New Ironsides* and *Housatonic* in the latter years of the war. Thanks to his persistent experiments, Holland emerged head and shoulders above his contemporary submarine pioneers: Garrett (Britain), Nordenfeldt (Sweden), Goubet and Dupuy de Lôme (France), and Peral (Spain). After a long succession of prototypes throughout the 1880s there emerged the *Holland VII* of 1895 and the *Holland VIII* of 1900. The latter was the forerunner of every non-nuclear submarine still in service in the 1980s: a pressure hull surrounded by flooding ballast tanks for submerging and surfacing; an air-breathing engine for running on the surface and elec-

tric motors for running submerged; and a bow torpedo tube.

These vital developments in *materiel* did not come about in isolation, prompted solely by the need to copy European models. They were matched by an ever-deepening professionalism in the US Navy's infrastructure, in which the leading lights were Stephen Bleecker Luce and his far more famous *protégé,* Alfred Thayer Mahan. Luce (1827-1917) had published a textbook on seamanship before commanding *Pontiac* while supporting Sherman's capture of Charleston in February 1865. After serving as commandant of midshipmen at the US Naval Academy, Annapolis, Luce became the foremost champion of a college for advanced naval studies, and was appointed first president of the US Naval War College when this was founded at Newport, Rhode Island, in October 1884. This splendid institution became a model of its kind for other navies; and it was also Luce who appointed Captain Mahan as lecturer in naval history.

Mahan (1840-1914) succeeded Luce as president of the Naval War College in 1886. He had also served during the Civil War, on blockade duty, but will always be remembered for his classic studies of sea power – *The Influence of Sea Power upon History, 1660-1783* (1890); *The Influence of Sea Power upon the French Revolution and Empire* (1892); biographies of Farragut (1892) and Nelson (1897); *Sea Power in its Relation to the War of 1812* (1905); and *The Major Operations of the Navies in the War of American Independence* (1913).

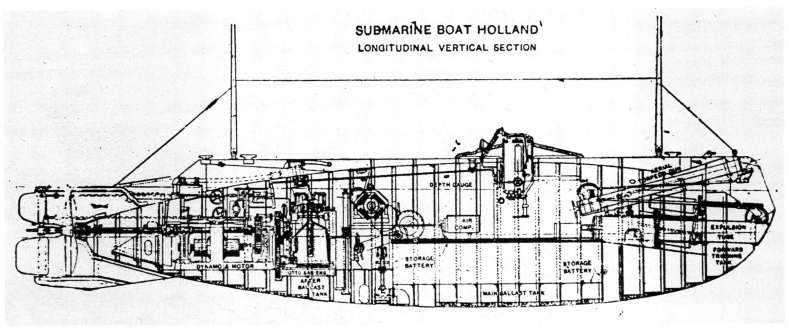

SUBMARINE BOAT HOLLAND
LONGITUDINAL VERTICAL SECTION

These masterpieces earned Mahan worldwide fame in his lifetime and entitle him to be remembered as the Clausewitz of naval theory (though Mahan's scholarship and clarity of style are infinitely superior to the unfinished works of the Prussian). Mahan's most famous doctrine, traced through every era in naval history, was that of the *fleet in being:* the outnumbered, perhaps even insignificant naval force which, by merely existing as a potential threat, prevents a more powerful enemy from deploying his full naval strength as he would. The exploits of the Confederate Navy between 1861 and 1865 had alone offered convincing proof of this.

The US Navy's continued advances both in *materiel* and in professional studies took place in a period of extended *détente* with the old enemy, Britain. Though postwar US governments accepted that the Confederate raiders of the Civil War had not been built or sustained with British governmental approval, American claims for postwar compensation by Britain were politely but firmly maintained. The result was an extension of the common sense which had resolved the 'Trent Incident' of November 1861. Both

cases, American and British, were submitted to international arbitration at Geneva in 1872, British liabilities being assessed at £3,100,000 – and both fully and promptly paid. The same solution was chosen for the next falling-out between the United States and Britain. This occurred in 1895, when President Grover Cleveland's administration cited the Monroe Doctrine during a boundary dispute between Venezuela and British Guiana. On this occasion the arbitrators decided in Britain's favor.

The inevitable result of continued equal and amicable relations with Britain was the sharpening of American imperial ambitions in the Pacific, which received their most disagreeable outlet in the Spanish-American War of 1898. The cause of the war was a Cuban revolt against Spanish rule, and American outrage against Spanish atrocities committed on the rebels – the said outrage being deliberately fanned for the sake of increased circulation by William Randolph Hearst, king of the popular press. Then, on 15 February, the US battleship *Maine* blew up and sank in Havana harbor. The disaster could quite easily have been spontaneous

A US Navy hallmark has always been the extraction of maximum utility from every class of ship by virtue of long-term service. This is the USS *Pensacola*, already obsolete less than 20 years after completion but serving as flagship of the Mediterranean squadron, at Alexandria in 1886.

Right: Heavy metal for the Pacific theater – 'Indiana' class battleship USS *Oregon* (BB.3) sets out from New York on the long haul round Cape Horn, bound for Manila in the Philippines, on 12 October 1898. Like her sister-ships *Indiana* and *Massachusetts*, she carried a main armament of four 13-inch guns in centerline turrets, with a secondary armament of eight 8-inch guns.

ammunition explosion (a tragedy known to all battleship navies down to and including the Second World War), but Hearst's newspapers shrieked accusations of Spanish sabotage. The fact that Spain apologized unreservedly and offered all sympathy, plus practical suggestions for resolving the crisis, went for nothing: the real American goal was not Cuba but the Spanish Philippines, on China's doorstep. On 21 April 1898, President William McKinley approved the Congressional resolution for armed intervention.

Meanwhile, bellicose Assistant Navy Secretary 'Teddy' Roosevelt had, without any authorization, briefed the commander of the US Pacific Squadron to move from Hawaii to Hong Kong. Thence, as soon as he heard that war with Spain had been declared, he was to descend on Manila and attack the Spanish fleet. Commodore George Dewey (1827-1917) had served under Farragut during the capture of New Orleans in 1862 and had a distinguished Civil War career. After running the gauntlet of Forts Jackson and St

Philip he was not deterred by the prospect of the Spanish batteries commanding Manila Bay, and sailed from Hong Kong with his six cruisers on 25 April. Shortly after midnight on 1 May, Dewey sailed past the outermost forts, ignored the shore batteries and headed straight for the ramshackle fleet.

Rarely, if ever, can American warships have had softer opponents. Admiral Montojo had seven ships in all, only three of them armored, and one a hulk which could only move under tow. So far from being drawn up in line of battle, Montojo had anchored close inshore to save as many of his crewmen as possible when the moment came to abandon ship. Dewey's chosen tactics were redolent of Civil War ironclad experience. Instead of anchoring to slug it out ship to ship, he made five slow runs past his victims, retiring to send the American crews to breakfast to give the smoke a chance to clear. It was typical of this war that Dewey went into US naval legend for his perfectly natural order to his gunnery officer on the eve of the first attack-

ing pass: 'You may fire when you are ready, Gridley.' By noon, what was left of Montojo's fleet surrendered, Spanish casualties totaling 381 in exchange for eight Americans lightly wounded and an overweight American chief engineer dead from heatstroke after collapsing below decks.

The Battle of Manila Bay established Dewey as the greatest American naval hero since Farragut, but ironically it was not for the battle but for its aftermath that Dewey deserved the fullest praise. He had no troops. He could not land to capture Manila. All he could do was stay on station, waging a magnificent game of bluff, until General Merritt arrived with an American expeditionary force. It took *14 weeks* before the troops arrived; landed; fought a brisk skirmish (six Americans and 49 Spaniards dead); and accepted the surrender of Manila on 13 August. The hardest fighting in this 'splendid little war' (as Secretary of State John Hay expressed it to Roosevelt) was in the Cuban theater, where 509 American troops were killed in battle and 1,800 died of disease. The big naval victory of the Cuban theater was the Battle of Santiago on 3 July 1898, won by Commodore William T. Sampson (1840-1902). Santiago was Manila Bay reversed, with Sampson's squadron destroying that of Admiral Cervera as it tried to break out; the victory made possible the American invasion of Puerto Rico on 25 July, which clinched the American victory.

However squalid the circumstances which had precipitated the conflict, the Spanish-American War of 1898 had one unanswerable result. Thanks mainly to the prowess of her Navy, the United States was now a global power, having gained not only Spanish withdrawal from Cuba but from the Philippines (in return for an inducement of $20 million paid to Spain). The United States also gained Guam in the Marianas and

Below: Victory review in New York Harbor (21 August 1898) after the defeat of Spain. *Left to right:* cruiser *New York*, battleships *Iowa* and *Oregon*.

Above: Rare photograph of American gunners during the Battle of Santiago (3 July 1898).

Puerto Rico in the Caribbean. The newly-acquired Philippines immediately proved their worth by serving as the advance base for the American forces which joined in the international force sent to crush the Boxer Rising in China (July-August 1900).

Even before the American successes in the Spanish War of 1898 had been fairly won, it had always been clear that the United States would never be able to enjoy a free hand in the exploitation of China, whether politically or economically. Apart from the British with

Above: View from the USS *Oregon* of the victors of Santiago during the victory review.

A trio of US pre-Dreadnoughts. *Top:* USS *Maine* (BB.10) as completed in 1902.
Above: USS *Kearsarge* (BB.5), with her imaginative but unworkable superimposition of co-axial 8-inch turrets atop the main 13-inch turrets.

Right: Superb shot of USS *Connecticut* (BB.18) at full speed in 1907.

their base at Hong Kong, there were the Russians at Port Arthur and Vladivostok, the Germans at Tsingtau – and, newest entrants of all, the newly-reconstituted Japanese Empire, making use of the latest European models to be ready to take on all rivals for the domination of China by land and sea. The decks were cleared by the Russo-Japanese War of 1904-5, in which the shattering defeat of Russian ambitions in the Far East left Japan – an ally of Britain since 1902 – as the most potent rival of the US Pacific Fleet. But Japan was not the only naval rival to the United States. On the Atlantic front, the Anglo-German naval building race, measured primarily in numbers of new battleships, was already fast accelerating by 1905. For the US Navy, faced with potential naval rivals from both East and West, there could be no withdrawal now from its costly 'two-ocean' status.

Thanks largely to the excellent groundwork of shipbuilders like Charles H. Cramp, the US Navy adapted with comparative ease to the radically improved battleship concept brought in by the British with HMS *Dreadnought* (1906). American naval designers – like their new Japanese rivals – also declined to ape the British and Germans and start building costly squadrons of the new 'battle-cruiser' type. These lightly-armored super-cruisers, armed with battleship-sized guns, were designed to annihilate enemy raiders and cruiser squadrons scouting ahead of the battle fleet, and 'take their place in the line'

to augment, when required, the fire-power of the battle fleet. Both American and Japanese sensed the fallacy (as propounded by the British Admiral Fisher) that 'speed is armor.' There could be no substitute for adequate armored protection, which made the *fast battleship* the ideal choice.

When Britain, France and Japan went to war with Germany in August 1914, the US Navy had eight Dreadnought battleships completed and two more building. This gave a clear lead over the Japanese battle fleet, with its six Dreadnoughts and two hybrid 'semi-Dreadnoughts' completed and two building. With the might of the British Grand Fleet holding the German High Seas Fleet in check (29 British Dreadnoughts and battle-cruisers against 20 German) the Pacific and Atlantic wings of the US Navy seemed safe enough. Though Japan clearly had her eyes on Germany's Pacific Island territories, Japan would never be given unrestricted play by her British ally. Even if, by some unimaginable chance, the German High Seas Fleet managed to defeat the Grand Fleet, this could hardly be achieved with the High Seas Fleet left intact. By any reckoning, American neutrality seemed to be the ideal course for the US Navy in 1914.

In fact this was not the case, and there were three reasons why not.

In 1914 the one factor under-estimated by all naval powers, belligerent and neutral alike, was an unknown one: the extent of the change about to be made in naval warfare by the ocean-going submarine, as demonstrated by Germany's U-boat fleet. On the high seas

the raiding submarine – unable to disembark prize crews or give full warning to its victim without exposing itself to mortal danger – was about to bring total war into being in the naval dimension. American failure to recognize this, and how it must result in loss of American life at sea, meant that once Germany resorted to fully unrestricted submarine warfare American entry into the war could only be a matter of time.

The second reason why American neutrality worked against the US Navy's best interests was even harder to see in August 1914. This lay in the pioneer field of naval aviation, in which the United States had made a promising start in 1910-12. It was an American pilot (Eugene Ely) who had made the first successful take-off from, and subsequently the first landing on, a warship fitted with a flight-deck. This had been achieved during an anxious prewar interlude when there were rumors that Germany was experimenting with spying aircraft, which

would fly off Atlantic liners and reconnoiter the American coast – a prospect not to be borne. American experiments with naval aviation were suspended with the proclamation of American neutrality; and when the US Navy did enter the war it found itself at least five years behind its allies in aircraft-carrier development.

The third reason was, perhaps, the most obvious in 1914: the fact that a neutral US Navy would not be accumulating the vital combat experience being amassed by its allies and likeliest enemies. Nor, on a peace-time footing, could the pace of American naval construction hope to match that of the combatant powers. As a result, the immediate contribution of the US Navy, after the United States joined the Allies on 6 April 1917, was painfully limited. The US Navy had never had to undergo the humiliating experience of being a poor relation in its entire existence, and it was not an easy experience to live with.

Eugene B. Ely shortly after landing on the cruiser USS *Pennsylvania* on 18 January 1911, before he took off again and landed safely ashore. Despite this historic 'first', the US Navy lagged behind the British and Japanese in naval aviation development until the 1920s.

The fact that Anglo-American naval collaboration worked out superbly in 1917-18 was due to the high tact and ready diplomacy displayed by the American naval commanders in European waters. Rear-Admiral William S. Sims (1858-1936) was 'Commander of the US Naval Forces Operating in European Waters.' His task, coming under the British Admiral Sir Lewis Bayly, based on Queenstown, Ireland, was to collaborate in the provision of Atlantic convoy escorts against the U-boats. Admiral Hugh Rodman (1959-1940) commanded the American Dreadnought battle squadron which joined the ranks of the British Grand Fleet, under the overall British command of Admiral Sir David Beatty. As an element of the Grand Fleet the American force was designated '6th Battle Squadron,' adopting British methods of signalling and fire control. The original battleships of 6th Battle Squadron (BatDiv 6, in US naval parlance) were *New York* (flag), *Florida*, *Wyoming* and *Delaware*.

It was with the fully-justified pride in faith kept and a job well done that Rodman's squadron deployed with its Grand Fleet comrades, on 21 November 1918, to receive the German High Seas Fleet as it came steaming duly west to surrender off the Firth of Forth. The German naval threat to American sea power had been destroyed – to all appearances, for ever. The Japanese naval threat continued to grow. How the peacetime naval powers could achieve a mutually satisfactory balance of strength – assuming such a feat were possible – remained to be seen.

Opposite, top: The amazing capacity of American warship production. In the summer of 1918, less than three weeks from laying-down to launch, the destroyer DD.139 (USS *Ward*) prepares to take the water.
Above: Scene of bleak discomfort on the exposed bridge of a US destroyer in the First World War.
Below: Over there – the destroyer USS *Stockton* (DD.73) in British waters.

At the time of Pearl Harbor in December 1941 the US Navy had 112 submarines in commission with another 65 completed. These are all of the 'New "S"' class, launched in 1937-38: USS *Stingray* (SS.186), *Sturgeon* (SS.187), *Salmon* (SS.182) and *Seal* (SS.183), exercising with the Battle Force in 1939. All four survived the Second World War.

groups operating independently of the main battle fleet. The big question for the US Navy was whether its remaining allocated carrier tonnage should be taken up with a few more large carriers, or several smaller ones. The disappointing performance of the lightweight *Ranger* (launched in 1933) tipped the scale in favor of larger carriers (*Yorktown* and *Enterprise*, launched in 1936). After one last experiment with the light-carrier format with *Wasp* (launched in 1939) the carrier type chosen for the US Navy was the 'medium-heavy', 27,000-ton 'Essex' class, the first of which were ordered in the 1940 Construction Program. But none of the 'Essex' class carriers was ready for service before Japan attacked the United States in December 1941. Nor were the first of the fast 16-inch gun battleships ('North Carolina' and 'South Dakota' classes) ordered in the 1937 and 1938 Programs. Ironically, these new battleships solved the problem of getting a full battery of 16-inch guns into 35,000 tons displacement (by using triple instead of twin turret mountings) long after the Washington Treaty was dead in spirit as well as in letter.

In its two years and three months of wartime neutrality before Pearl Harbor, the US Navy benefited enormously from British wartime experience in the Narrow Seas, Atlantic, Arctic and Mediterranean. The two most obvious of these British-inspired benefits were sonar, for detecting submerged submarines, and radar for surface and air surveillance, invented by the British and perfected by American technology. The British also served as guinea-pigs in the hitherto unknown field of how modern warships would stand up to expert air attack, showing that no anti-aircraft battery of rapid-firing guns could really be considered sufficient. The loss of the British carrier *Courageous* in September 1939 and of *Glorious* in June 1940, respectively to U-boat and surface attack, showed the supreme vulnerability of carriers when exposed without adequate anti-submarine screening or heavy ship support. Finally, the British search for auxiliary air cover which could be extended to cover convoys produced the new concept of the escort carrier, converted from merchant ships. When mass-produced by American shipyards with their world-beating capacity, escort carriers became the means by which the fleet carriers were completely freed for purely offensive instead of supportive opera-

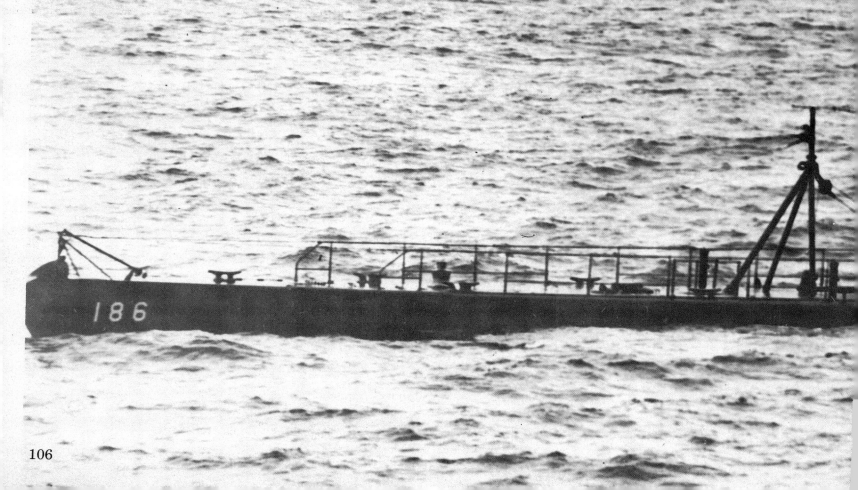

tions. *Long Island,* the US Navy's first escort carrier (CVE), was completed over six months before Pearl Harbor, at the beginning of June 1941.

Setting aside these crucial debts to British technology and combat experience, in the renewal of basic warship types the US Navy had been far better served than the Royal Navy during the 1930s. (Having a 'Navy-minded' President in Franklin D. Roosevelt, who as a rising young politician had served as Assistant Navy Secretary, was an invaluable boon.) In the seven years between Roosevelt's first inauguration as President in 1933 and the outbreak of the European war in September 1939, successive Construction Programs ordered a total of four aircraft-carriers, six battleships, three heavy cruisers, 13 light cruisers, 83 destroyers and 38 submarines. But the emergency 1940 Program – cast in the light of the German bid for mastery in Europe – alone ordered nine battleships, 17 carriers, eight heavy cruisers, 38 light cruisers, 196 destroyers and 73 submarines. This was virtually *double* the *combined total* of the Programs *for the previous seven years,* most of whose ships were completed in time to help bear the brunt of

the Japanese offensive in 1941-42. The new ships coming forward in the last five years of peace before Pearl Harbor were ample to replace those lost in the US Navy's first year of war: two battleships, four carriers, five heavy cruisers, two light cruisers, 27 destroyers and eight submarines.

The assurance of ample warship replacements, however, only spelled comfort for the future; they could do nothing to halt the

Above: Fine shot of the Battle Force at sea in 1939. It was not until the Pacific Fleet's battle line was liquidated at Pearl Harbor that the new carrier arm became the US Navy's dominant arm.

The hecatomb of battleships at Pearl Harbor, with smoke belching from USS *Tennessee* (BB.43) at left. A small boat heads in to pluck a survivor from the upperworks of USS *West Virginia* (BB.48) at right foreground. Excellent counter-flooding work saved the 'Weavie' from capsizing, allowing her to settle on the bottom on an even keel. Both battleships were repaired and returned to service in 1943-44.

initial run of Japanese victories in 1941-42. Nothing remotely approaching the breadth of the Japanese offensive – from Wake Island and the Gilberts in the Central Pacific, south to the Dutch East Indies, New Guinea and the Solomons, and west to Malaya and Burma – had ever been dreamed of by American strategists. Still very much battleship-orientated, American prewar naval strategy had envisaged a 'one-front' Japanese offensive, with the Philippines high on the list of likely targets. Once committed to such an offensive, the Japanese could then be taken in flank by the advance of the US Pacific Fleet from Hawaii into the Central Pacific, to fight a predominantly battleship action somewhere in the Philippine Sea. But this scenario was liquidated on 7 December 1941, when the six carriers of the Japanese task force sank or crippled every one of the US Pacific Fleet's eight battleships at Pearl Harbor. The often-cited British carrier attack on the Italian battle fleet at Taranto on 11 November 1940 pales into insignificance by comparison with Pearl Harbor. For the only time in all naval history, one of the world's most powerful navies had been forced onto the defensive by a major disaster, suffered on the first day of hostilities, with not one of the enemy warships responsible having been sighted. This was a humiliating fate for America's much-vaunted 'Two-Ocean Navy.'

Because of the simultaneous German declaration of war on the United States, there could be no question of rushing instant reinforcements from the Atlantic to the Pacific Fleet. Only driblet reinforcements could

The cruiser USS *Phoenix* (CVL.46) passes the funeral pyre of the battle line at Pearl Harbor.
Inset: USS *Nevada* (compare with pp. 104-105), beached and burning after failing to escape to the open sea during the Japanese attack.

be spared from the Atlantic, where the battle against Germany's U-boats was necessarily left to the hard-pressed Royal Navy in 1942. In the Pacific, therefore, the traditional concept of an American battle fleet supported by carriers was shattered for ever by the Pearl Harbor disaster. Only a handful of American carriers and cruisers remained, apparently the flimsiest of weapons with which to oppose the Japanese Combined Fleet at the peak of its strength.

Yet they were just enough. Within six months of Pearl Harbor, two major Japanese offensives had been frustrated by carrier battles in which, for the first time, neither fleet ever sighted the other. And in these battles – the Coral Sea (May 1942) and Midway (June 1942) – the Japanese superiority in carriers was wiped out. For this reversal, Japanese over-confidence and un-

realistic planning played a major part. But there can be no detracting from the US Navy's achievement against all odds, for which five American admirals claim an enduring share of fame.

Ernest J. King (1878-1956) was the man at the top, directly under Roosevelt as Commander-in-Chief of the US Armed Forces. In the inevitable command changes after Pearl Harbor, King was advanced from C-in-C

Atlantic Fleet (CINCLANT) to Commander-in-Chief, US Fleet (COMUNCH). A hard-core professional who never lost faith that the US Navy would come through to win the war, King's greatest achievement was in picking the man who would start the job by restoring faith and fighting efficiency to the US Pacific Fleet: Admiral Chester W. Nimitz (1885-1966).

Patient, shrewd, with all the warmer human qualities lacking in the more forbidding character of King, Nimitz had the gift of extracting the maximum results from the minimum resources – human and *materiel*. He was the ideal commander to take up King's brief in December 1941: 'Hold what you've got and hit them where you can.' Few commanders ever showed more skill in exploiting that most unpredictable of factors in war: the enemy's mistakes.

The gutsy and ebullient William F. Halsey (1882-1959) embodied the fighting spirit of the US carrier arm, with his slogans, 'Before we've finished with 'em, the Japanese language will be spoken only in hell!' and 'Kill Japs, kill Japs, kill more Japs!' He commanded the carrier raid which on 18 April 1942 launched Army B-25s to bomb Tokyo – the most convincing proof possible that the US Pacific Fleet was still a force to be reckoned with. The Tokyo Raid deprived Halsey of the chance of joining the fray in the Coral Sea battle (4-8 May 1942), which foiled the Japanese conquest of Port Moresby and saved a vital foothold in New Guinea for the

Right: USS *Enterprise* (CV.6) recovering Dauntless strike aircraft off Guadalcanal in December 1942, with USS *Saratoga* (CV.3) in background. Three other aircraft can be seen above the tailfin of the Dauntless in foreground.
Below: A Hellcat of VF-1 'Top Hat' Squadron, poised for take-off from the second *Yorktown* (CV.10) during the 'Great Marianas Turkey Shoot' in June 1944.

Allies. When sickness forced Halsey ashore on the eve of the supreme trial at Midway, his choice of successor proved to be one of the greatest naval tacticians of the new carrier era.

Frank Jack Fletcher (1885-1973) was, with Halsey, the foremost carrier task force commander in the hit-and-run raids on the Japanese perimeter, ordered by Nimitz in the spring of 1942. Fletcher won the Battle of the Coral Sea and, until his flagship *Yorktown* was mortally damaged, commanded the US carrier ambush on the Japanese at Midway on 4 June 1942. Thus deprived of effective command with the Midway battle still hanging in the balance, Fletcher wisely decided to conform to the movements of Halsey's chosen successor, Raymond A. Spruance (1886-1969), who until Halsey's illness had commanded the cruiser element in Halsey's task Force. Thanks to the combined judgment of Fletcher and Spruance and the supreme gallantry of the aircrews of *Yorktown, Enterprise* and *Hornet,* four of the six Japanese carriers which had struck at Pearl Harbor were sunk and carrier parity between the American and Japanese navies precariously restored.

After Midway came the long agony of Guadalcanal (August 1942-February 1943): a merciless battle of attrition in the central Solomon Islands, with both navies at full stretch to supply their troops locked in combat on Guadalcanal. The campaign was fought to the limit of endurance, with two more daytime carrier battles (Eastern Solomons on 24 August and Santa Cruz on 26 October), and a string of vicious night actions between the rival cruiser/destroyer forces. By November 1942 the US Pacific Fleet was down to its last operational carrier, *Enterprise. Wasp* and *Hornet* had followed *Yorktown* (lost at Midway) and *Lexington* (lost at the Coral Sea). Both sides finally committed battleships to the Guadalcanal night fighting, with the new American *Washington* and *South Dakota* finally tipping the balance on the night of 14-15 November 1942. From then on the Japanese were reduced to supplying their army on Guadalcanal with clandestine night runs, having lost the equivalent of an entire peacetime fleet since the

Previous pages: Hellcat fighters (foreground) and Avenger strike aircraft ranged for take-off on a US carrier.
Left: The first two US fleet carriers lost in the Pacific War were USS *Lexington* (CV.2) at Coral Sea in May 1942, and *(below)* the first *Yorktown* (CV.5) at Midway in June 1942. By the end of the year *Wasp* and *Hornet* had followed, both sunk off Guadalcanal; with *Saratoga* damaged, this briefly left *Enterprise* as the only operational US fleet carrier in the Pacific.

Right: The two forward turrets of the main battery: 14-inch guns in triple mountings. *Opposite:* The heavy guns of the vital anti-aircraft umbrella – 5-inch AA guns at exercise.

Above: Devastator torpedo-bombers prepare for launch from *Enterprise* during the Battle of Midway (June 1942). Bereft of close fighter cover, slow and vulnerable, only four of the aircraft in this picture came back.

start of the campaign: two battleships, one carrier, five cruisers, 12 destroyers and eight submarines. When this last desperate venture failed, the Japanese High Command accepted the inevitable and ordered the evacuation of Guadalcanal.

The Guadalcanal victory was an extraordinary achievement by the US Navy. The campaign was fought and won on two levels: the Navy's determination not to leave the Marine garrison to its fate, and the attempt to maintain naval air cover until the troops

on the ground had conquered enough real estate for land-based air cover to take over. The inevitable result was to deprive the US carriers of their most valuable asset — operating from 'no fixed address' — thus exposing them to heavy losses from Japanese submarine and carrier attack. The victory was another triumph for Nimitz, who refused to despair when American prospects seemed darkest; and for Halsey, appointed by Nimitz as Commander-in-Chief, South Pacific (ComSoPac).

After Guadalcanal, Halsey remained as ComSoPac to direct the dogged advance up the Solomons chain which culminated in the invasion of Bougainville on 31 October 1943. Spruance was meanwhile appointed by Nimitz to command the 5th Fleet: the ever-increasing concentration of new carriers ('Essex' and 'Independence' classes) which arrived in the Pacific from the autumn of 1943. Backed by an armada of storeships and tankers to remain at sea for weeks on end, withdrawing between attacks to advance bases created from empty coral atolls, the 5th Fleet launched the long-awaited break-in to the Central Pacific with its attack on the Gilberts in November 1943. The Marshalls followed in February 1944 and then on 16 June 1944 the 5th Fleet covered the invasion of Saipan in the Marianas, which brought on the last great carrier battle of the Pacific War: the Battle of the Philippine Sea (19-20

June 1944).

The Philippine Sea was Spruance's greatest tactical triumph, in which he refused to expose the Saipan invasion fleet and waited for the Japanese to come to him – to be shot down in scores by the 5th Fleet's carrier fighters. It was the swansong of the Japanese carrier arm, which went into battle with 430 aircraft against 891 and came out with only 35 – the 'Great Marianas Turkey Shoot,' as the Americans exultingly dubbed the engagement. After the Philippine Sea, the last operational Japanese carriers were toothless tigers, useful only as decoys in the extraordinary plan concocted for the defense of the Philippines: 'Sho-Go'.

Above: Top brass on Saipan – the leading UD admirals of the Second World War, with Fleet Admiral 'Ernie' King (COMINCH) at center.

Below: Enterprise at speed during the Battle of Midway, with a cruiser of the screen at right of picture.

This involved using empty Japanese carriers as decoys to lure away the massed American fleet carriers, exposing the American invasion fleet, as it lay off the invasion beaches, to a devastating attack by the Japanese battleships and cruisers. The result was the Battle of Leyte Gulf (23-25 October 1944), the greatest sea battle of all time, in which 244 ships on both sides were engaged.

Halsey had returned to sea for the assault on the Philippines, replacing Spruance in command of what was redesignated the '3rd Fleet.' That the Japanese decoy plan came perilously close to success was due to Halsey's aggressive desire to pursue and engage the enemy, giving the Japanese battle fleet a clear run through San Bernadino Strait. The morning of 25 October found the escort carriers of Admiral Kinkaid's 7th Fleet, screening the invasion fleet's northern flank, forced to run for dear life from the battleships until the latter, fearing renewed carrier air attack, turned and withdrew. Halsey's conduct earned a sharp rebuke from Nimitz, who intervened with a direct order to Halsey to cease his pursuit of the Japanese carriers and support 7th Fleet. Though Halsey's carriers duly caught and massacred the Japanese decoy carriers off Cape Engano, the 3rd Fleet's 'Battle Line' failed to intercept the retreating Japanese battleships. For all that, Leyte Gulf was a decisive American victory. It secured the vital beach-head for the reconquest of the Philippines and broke the back of what was left of the Japanese Fleet. At Leyte Gulf the Japanese lost three battleships, four carriers, ten cruisers and nine destroyers; American losses were one carrier, two escort carriers and three destroyers.

Though Leyte Gulf was the last battle fought by the Japanese Fleet, the 3rd/5th Fleet had one prolonged ordeal in store. This was the attempt to decimate the American warships with attacks by *kamikazes:* suicide aircraft, the pledged watchword of whose pilots was 'one plane, one warship.' The *kamikaze* attacks reached their zenith in

Right: Kamikaze ordeal off Okinawa, 28 April 1945. Too close for the AA guns to bear, a bomb-laden Zero aims for the side of USS *Missouri* (BB.63). This attack was unsuccessful, the Zero crashing into the sea only a few feet short of its target.

April-May 1945 as Spruance's 5th Fleet covered the invasion of Okinawa. All in all, 5th Fleet beat off 1,809 *kamikaze* sorties, shooting down 930 aircraft in the process. Though no American carriers were sunk, 5th Fleet suffered 17 ships sunk and 198 damaged, including 12 fleet carriers and three battleships. In this ordeal the support of the newly-formed British Pacific Fleet, operating with 5th Fleet as 'Task Force 57,' was welcomed in most generous terms by both Spruance and Nimitz. No more than a standard American task force in strength, the British Pacific Fleet readily adjusted to American command and signalling techniques. The wheel had indeed come full circle since the American battle fleet had formed a lone squadron in Beatty's Grand Fleet in the last year of the First World War.

After Okinawa, Halsey returned to begin the softening-up of the Japanese home islands for 'Olympic,' the invasion of Kyushu scheduled for November 1945. The strength of 3rd Fleet, as it sortied from Leyte on its last campaign in July 1945, was ten fleet and six light carriers, eight battleships, 19 cruisers, and over 60 destroyers – a far cry from the threadbare force which had sailed into immortality at Midway barely three years before. What proved to be the last month of the Pacific War was abruptly cut short by the atomic bombs which fell on Hiroshima on 6 August and Nagasaki on 9 August. When the Japanese made their surrender on the deck of the battleship USS *Missouri* in Tokyo Bay on 2 September, the triumph of the US Navy was complete.

Below: 'Independence' class light fleet carrier *Langley* (CVL.27), with fleet carrier *Ticonderoga* (CV.14) in background.

6: SHIELD OF THE FREE WORLD 1945-1984

With the defeat of Japan in the late summer of 1945 – 170 years since the Continental Congress had first set about organising a Patriot navy with which to fight the British at sea – the US Navy stood revealed as the mightiest instrument of sea power in world history. Perhaps the most amazing aspect of this growth to world supremacy is the fact that it was largely crammed into the last two of those 170 years. The US Navy and the Royal Navy reached their most exact point of balance in the spring of 1943, before the flood of new American carriers entered service. It was in 1943 that US warships, for the last time, served in European waters under British supreme command – when units of the US Atlantic Fleet reinforced the British Home Fleet against the threat of the German battleship *Tirpitz*.

The pace of the US Navy's wartime expansion was staggering. In June 1942, the month of Midway, the US Navy had numbered 5,612 ships of all types and a manpower strength (including Marines and Coast Guards) of 843,096. In June 1945, it numbered 67,952 ships and a manpower strength of 4,031,097 – and it was still expanding in preparation for the invasion of Japan, which, judged by the time it had taken to reconquer the Philippines, was not expected to be completed until the summer of 1946.

The unexpectedly early end of the Pacific War in 1945 was not followed by the classic peacetime levelling-off and downturn in American naval development. No sooner had Japan surrendered than American sea power was given new impetus by three completely novel phenomena. The first of these, born of the war, was technological: the urgent need to adjust naval equipment and strategy to the advent of the atom bomb, jet aircraft and helicopter. The second was political. The hostile attitude of the Soviet Union, the imposition of Communist regimes under Soviet control on the whole of eastern Europe, and the Communist victory in China were to American eyes, the manifestation of a new global threat as great as that so recently posed by Germany, Italy and Japan. The third was the vacuum caused by the impending dissolution of the British Empire, starting with Indian independence in 1948, and the accelerated postwar shrinkage of the hitherto supreme Royal Navy.

Britain was bankrupt and economically ravaged after six years of war; the British economy in 1945-46 was only saved by a massive American dollar loan. One of Britain's most urgent postwar needs was to get as many men as possible out of the Services and into the factories. Between 1945 and 1948 the Royal Navy's manpower fell from 863,000 to 147,000 and there was a massive shake-out in warships of prewar vintage: 10 old battleships and a battle-cruiser, 20 cruisers, 61 destroyers and 77 corvettes. Britain's entire fleet of 37 escort carriers, built in the United States, was handed back under the terms of Lend-Lease. On VJ-Day in 1945, the overall strength of the British Pacific Fleet had consisted of four battleships, 10 fleet carriers, nine escort carriers, 11 cruisers, 40 destroyers and 29 submarines. Three years later, the strength *of the entire British Fleet,* in all waters, had dwindled to four battleships, eight carriers, 17 cruisers, 52 destroyers and 34 submarines (excluding the Reserve). By 1950 the British strength in the Pacific was a ghost of what it had been only five years before. The heaviest Royal Naval contribution to the United Nations fleet in the Korean War was one light fleet carrier.

This tremendous postwar run-down of the British Fleet confirmed that the mantle of global sea power *in strength* had passed to the US Navy, which in 1945 had over 3,600 named ships of all types, and thousands more bearing numbers only. The excellent prewar groundwork in modernising the American fleet meant that immediate postwar disposals (1945-48) weeded out fewer heavy ships than in the Royal Navy: seven old battleships to the British ten, 11 escort carriers to the British 37, 11 cruisers to the British 20. Even after 132 old American destroyers had been sold or scrapped between 1945 and 1948, this still left over 500 available for service.

Inevitably, therefore, the US Navy played a dominant role in the crucial operations in Korea of 1950-51. When Communist North Korea invaded South Korea at 11 points in June 1950, the force best placed to rush support to the faltering South Koreans was the US 7th Fleet of Vice-Admiral Arthur Struble, based on Japan. Struble was unusually well qualified for the job. He had been chief of staff during the US naval planning for the invasion of Normandy in 1944, commanded an attack group at Leyte Gulf, and had been promoted commander of US amphibious forces in the Pacific in September 1945. He now became the first American admiral required to fight a naval war exclusively tailored to the demands of the land forces, with no enemy naval chal-

The awesome streamlined bulk of USS *Ohio* (SSBN.726), the first of the Trident-firing giant ballistic missile submarines, commissioned in 1981. Each of these giants carries firing tubes for 24 Trident missiles with over ten warheads per missile. Trident's range (at over 4,000 miles (6,437 km) nearly double that of the earlier Poseidon) enables the 'Ohio' class ships to menace targets in the Soviet Union from waters where the Soviet anti-submarine fleet dare not venture. An 'Ohio' has a displacement greater than most light aircraft-carriers at 18,700 tons (18,999 tonnes) submerged.

lenge to meet – a far cry from the days of Guadalcanal, the Marianas and the Philippines in 1942-45. Korea was also the only war in which an American fleet has formed the core of a United Nations force called into being to resist aggression. The 7th Fleet off Korea was ably seconded by contingents from the British, Canadian, Australian, New Zealand, French and Dutch navies.

The naval war off Korea started promisingly enough for the UN naval forces, with the virtual elimination of North Korea's scanty coastal navy in the first weeks of the war (July-September 1950) by carrier air attacks and gun actions by surface warships. Over the following year, however, the dramatic swings of fortune on land finally took the form of a strategic stalemate. The further south the North Koreans advanced the heavier they were hammered by UN air attacks, with carriers playing an increasing role. Conversely, the further north the UN forces advanced, the harder it proved to give them adequate support. UN sea power (with the US 7th Fleet covering the Korean east coast and the other UN naval forces the west) enabled the UN counter-offensive of autumn 1950 to be speeded by two impressive amphibious 'hooks' behind the Communist lines, at Inchon (September) and Wonsan (October). UN advances north beyond the Yalu River, however, proved impossible to sustain, and

after another Communist assault was repelled in May 1951 armistice talks got warily under way at Kaesong. They were to drag on for another two years before the armistice ending the war was finally signed at Panmunjom, in July 1953.

For the US Navy, the legacy of Korea was a mixed one. The war confirmed the versatility of the big carrier as an 'all-arms' air support and strike force, able to provide fighter cover as well as tactical air/ground support. As in 1941-45, this applied both to amphibious landings and to subsequent operations ashore. The wisdom of 'mothballing' older ships (particularly carriers) was also proven. But Korea also showed that land targets within reach of naval gunfire can be far more economically destroyed by cruisers and battleships than by carrier aircraft. Expressed as 'cost effectiveness', shells are cheaper to make, store, and unleash on the enemy than piloted aircraft; the expenditure of radar-directed heavy shells is far less costly than that of shot-down sophisticated aircraft and trained aircrew.

One of the greatest paradoxes of the international naval scene since 1945 is that the United States, home of the world's most wasteful 'throw-away' consumer culture, has practised unequalled thrift with regard to its warships. Many years have to pass before an American warship is declared unfit for furth-

The old and the new in Korean waters (February 1952). In the center, USS *Rainier* (AE.5) pulls away after simultaneously replenishing the carrier USS *Antietam* (CV.36) and the 'Iowa' class battleship USS *Wisconsin* (BB.64).

Mothballed American destroyers, all capable of speedy return to front-line service, on the Pacific coast in July 1966. Preserving obsolescent ships instead of scrapping them has always been a prudent hallmark of the US Navy.

The guided missile frigate
USS *Oliver Hazard Perry*
(FFG.7), commissioned in
December 1977. She carries
40 Harpoon/Standard
surface/AA missiles, two
helicopters in the after
hangar, a 76mm gun, and
two triple torpedo tubes for
anti-submarine work – all-
round potential in a hull
displacing 3,605 tons (3,663
tonnes) at full load.

Scene on the flight deck of the amphibious warfare ship USS *Guam* (LPH.9) during the American intervention in Grenada (October 1983), with troop-carrying Chinook helicopter in background.

Pacific War veteran USS *Ticonderoga* (compare with pp. 101, 124) still very much in service in 1961, extensively rebuilt with a portside angled flight deck and fully-enclosed or 'hurricane' bow.

er service, and consigned for sale or scrap. The essence of the US Navy's postwar policy on warship strengths has always been to go, wherever possible, for the longest feasible service life through repeated modernisation. This again has presented a total contrast to British practice, and has remained unchanged for nearly four decades. When HMS *Victorious,* Britain's last wartime heavy fleet carrier, was phased out in 1968, the US Navy still had 13 wartime 'Essex' class carriers in service. Two of these were offered to the Royal Navy in 1981 by President Reagan's Government, alarmed at the apparent British determination to do away with carriers completely. (This was the year before the total insanity of Britain's carrier policy was exposed by the Falklands War.) The last British fleet carrier, HMS *Ark Royal,* was axed in 1978 – though she was ten years 'younger' than the first class of American postwar heavy carriers, the 'Midways'. At the time of going to press, in the spring of 1984, the 'Midway' class *Coral Sea* is undergoing a refit which will extend her operational career to no less than 50 years: 1945-1995.

On a far more modest but inevitably more controversial scale, the same has applied to the US Navy's battleships. Fifteen years on, the lessons of Korea were re-taught in the Vietnam War. In this conflict the US 7th Fleet provided offshore support for the South Vietnamese and American forces with six carriers (450 aircraft). By 1968, however, aircraft and aircrew losses to North Vietnamese anti-aircraft fire had become so costly that the US Army and Marine Corps – not the Navy – were urging the reactivation of the veteran battleship *New Jersey.* Over 1,000 targets hitherto accessible only to strike aircraft lay within the range of her 16-inch guns, which fired 5,688 rounds (com-

Above: A US Navy F-4B Phantom in a high-level bombing attack over Vietnam.

Right: The battleship USS *New Jersey* (BB.62) firing her full 16-inch broadside during her 1968-69 recommission for service in the Vietnam War.

USS *Long Beach* (CGN.9) was the first American cruiser designed since 1941; the world's first nuclear-powered surface warship; and the first surface warship armed with a guided-missile main battery. She was brought into service in September 1961.

June 1982: USS *Ticonderoga*, first ship of the newest American class of guided-missile cruisers, armed with the Aegis missile system, underway in the Gulf of Mexico.

The Combat Information Center (CIC) in USS *Ticonderoga*. Here are displayed the data gathered by the ship's four fixed-array AN/SPY 1A radars, revealing situations which might threaten the ship and the battle group she is designed to protect. The ship's weapons – AA and surface missiles, rapid-firing deck guns, anti-submarine torpedoes and rockets – are all directed and fired from the CIC.

pared with only 771 between 1943 and 1945) during her experimental recommission in 1968-69. It was calculated that the $21 million cost of her refit and recommission was equal to the value of six shot-down F4 Phantom aircraft. Within another ten years the heartfelt advocacy of former pilots was pressing for yet another return of *New Jersey* to active service, this time as a combined missile and big-gun platform. In this new guise her awesome silhouette appeared off the strife-torn coast of Beirut in the New Year of 1984, supporting the 6th Fleet's abortive 'peace-keeping' mission, hurling 16-inch shells across the Shouf Moutains onto rebel PLO gun positions.

Extending the operational careers of veter-

an warships past all known limits has gone hand in hand with a formidable inventiveness in new technologies and new ship types. This has been most obvious in the two mainstays of American sea power since 1945: the giant carrier and the submarine.

The big carrier was the natural legacy of the Pacific War in which, after 1942, the only American carriers lost were the lightweight 'Independence' class *Princeton* and five escort carriers. From this experience, American carrier doctrine argues that a big carrier stands a better chance of surviving submarine or air attack, and can also mount more anti-aircraft guns (or, latterly, missiles). More obviously, the bigger the carrier, the bigger (and better balanced) the air group can be. This means more fighters both for defense from air attacks, and for escorting attack missions flown by the carrier's strike aircraft. Big carriers also proved perfectly suited to operating the new jet aircraft of the postwar era, with their increased dead-weights and flying speeds. The first jet-powered carrier launch (of a McDonnell FH-1 Phantom) was made from *Coral Sea* in July 1946.

After a false start with *United States* (aborted in 1949) American heavy-carrier development was resumed in the light of

Sonar Technicians man their underwater watch stations at the console aboard the 'Los Angeles' class nuclear-powered attack submarine USS *La Jolla*.

Korean War experience. The result was the four-ship 'Forrestal' class (*Forrestal, Saratoga, Ranger,* and *Independence*), the first of which was ordered in 1952. These mighty ships, with their full-displacement of 78,000 tons, were the first post-1945 heavy carriers, designed and built specifically for operating jet aircraft. They gave the US Navy an entirely new strategic function: as a global vehicle for the American nuclear deterrent. Though the simultaneous development of the ballistic missile-firing submarine (SSBN) soon robbed the American carrier arm of a monopoly in nuclear 'clout', the Forrestals served as prototypes for the mightiest floating structures ever built by man: the nuclear-powered *Enterprise* which was commissioned in 1961 and ultimately the 91,500-ton *Nimitz* (commissioned 1975) and her successors.

Not content with transforming the role of the heavy fleet carrier, the US Navy was simultaneously achieving the same for its submarine arm. The end of the Pacific War had carried the American submarine arm to an unprecedented eminence. In the submarine 'Battle of the Pacific' against Japanese shipping, the US Navy's submarines – though only amounting to two percent of the total American naval strength in the Pacific, destroyed 61 percent of the Japanese merchant fleet. The ravages caused by the American submarines made it impossible for the Japanese to ship troops and supplies to the island garrisons menaced by the US carrier task forces, completely distrupted the internal sealanes of the Japanese Empire, and were a major factor in bringing about the early end of the war. They succeeded, in short, where Germany's U-boats had failed in the Atlantic, and the significance of this was not forgotten after the Japanese defeat.

American submarine development after 1945 was aimed at pushing the conventional diesel/electric submarine to the limit and to developing a practicable nuclear power plant. The first stage was perfecting a streamlined hull which would yield high submerged speeds. The now-familiar 'teardrop' or 'whale' shape was proven by the experimental *Albacore* (1953), the first submarine to break 30 knots when submerged. The first nuclear-powered submarines,

Stunning head-on shot of the 'super-carrier' USS *Carl Vinson* (CVN.70), third ship of the nuclear-powered 'Nimitz' class. With a deep-load displacement of 91,487 tons (92,951 tonnes), these carriers are the biggest warships of all time.

Poised for launch from the steam catapult: a Grumman F-14 Tomcat. This advanced 'swing-wing' all-weather fighter (the wings retract aft for high-speed flight) has a maximum speed of Mach 2.4.

USS *Enterprise*, the US Navy's first nuclear-powered 'super-carrier'. When completed in 1961 she was the largest floating structure ever built by man, but still took only 31 months from laying-down to launch.

Above: The first nuclear-powered aircraft carrier USS *Enterprise* (CVN-65) and USS *Tuxton* (CGN-35), the nuclear-powered 'Belknap' class cruiser.

the more powerful Poseidon missile with its multiple-warhead punch. But all were dwarfed by the 'Ohio' class giants, built to carry the Trident missile in 24 launching tubes: 18,700 tons submerged displacement and 560 feet in length, larger than most light aircraft-carriers of the Second World War.

The US Navy of the 1980s therefore has a greater range of major capacities than at any other time of technical peace. Its SSBNs and carriers have a crucial nuclear strike potential; in the conventional carrier task force role, its surface forces have retained all the versatility in support and strike potential, which their predecessors perfected in the Pacific War. Its 'hunter-killer' submarines, both nuclear and conventionally powered, maintain the triple task of enemy commerce destruction and enemy warship-hunting, both surface and submarine. Its amphibious capacity, with helicopter carriers and support ships, is one of the greatest assets of the North Atlantic Treaty Organisation in which the US Navy has played the dominant role since the formation of the Alliance in 1949.

The formation of NATO set the seal on the recasting of global sea power which had emerged from the Second World War. A NATO Supreme Command for the Atlantic (SACLANT) was established at Norfolk, Virginia, with the US 2nd Fleet and the Royal Navy undertaking joint responsibility for Europe's Atlantic lifeline. The former British paramountcy in the Mediterranean passed to the US 6th Fleet, with the US 7th Fleet continuing to watch the western Pacific and the US 3rd Fleet the eastern Pacific. This 'all-ocean' capability extends to the maintenance of powerful US forces in the Indian Ocean and approaches to the Persian Gulf.

Yet fellow-members of NATO have no grounds for complacency. The rise of a powerful Soviet fleet, with all essential capabilities matching those of the US Navy save in numbers and technological excellence, has proceeded unabated over the past 25 years. Soviet naval growth has not, however, been matched by similar efforts on the part of the US Navy's NATO allies, predominantly Britain. Even when all the capacities of the US Navy are listed, the combined NATO naval deployment has shrunk from 35 carriers and 440 destroyers and frigates in 1960 to 13 carriers and 333 destroyers and frigates in 1980. The day may yet come when the US Navy, increasingly the seaborne shield of the Free World, is called upon to shoulder a burden beyond even its mighty strength.

Nautilus (1955) and *Seawolf* (1956) retained a conventional submarine hull design, the full 'teardrop' hull being used in *Skipjack* (laid down in May 1956).

Long before the 'Skipjacks' had even been launched, however, it was clear that even more fundamental changes must be made. The shift of nuclear weapons delivery from conventional bombing aircraft to ballistic rocket missile threw a new burden on the US Navy: providing submarine launching-platforms for ballistic missiles which cannot — unlike land-based missile sites — be 'taken out' with the first enemy strike. This was achieved with the 'George Washingtons', first of the US Navy's SSBN fleet within a fleet, designed to lurk unseen in the ocean wastes with their batteries of Polaris missiles.

This development, modified and expanded to keep pace with the parallel advances in missile development, has produced warships which stagger the imagination. *George Washington,* commissioned in the same year as *Skipjack* (1959), displaced 6,888 tons to *Skipjack's* 3,513 tons. Their successors were the 'Ethan Allens' (7,880 tons), and the 'Benjamin Franklins' and 'Lafayettes' (8,250 tons), yielding a total of 41 SSBNs in service with the US Navy by the end of 1967. After less than a decade in service for the earlier SSBNs, they were being converted to carry

Previous page: The flight-deck crews take charge as an F-4 Phantom is towed across the flight deck of the 'Florrestal' class carrier USS *Ranger* (CV-61). *Above:* Three other Phantoms head downwind for recovery after another mission over Vietnam (1968).

Below: Lebanon, 1983: the US 6th Fleet re-embarks Marines from the dockside of Beirut as the 'peace-keeping' force is withdrawn.

Right: The deadly avenue of firing tubes for the Trident missiles of USS *Ohio*.

Bottom: Submarine USS *Nautilus*, which flashed the historic signal 'UNDERWAY ON NUCLEAR POWER' for the first time on 17 January 1955, predating the first Soviet nuclear-powered submarines by an estimated three years.

Index